A BOOK *of* PRAYER

A BOOK of PRAYER

FOR GAY AND LESBIAN CHRISTIANS

WILLIAM G. STOREY, D.M.S.

Professor Emeritus of Medieval Liturgy
and Church History

The University of Notre Dame

A Crossroad Book
The Crossroad Publishing Company
New York

The Crossroad Publishing Company
481 Eighth Avenue, New York, NY 10001

Printed in the United States of America

Library of Congress Cataloging-in-Publication Data
A book of prayer for gay & lesbian Christians / compiled and arranged by
    William G. Storey.
        p.   cm.
    ISBN 0-8245-1937-X (alk. paper)
    1. Gays – Prayer-books and devotions – English.   I. Storey, William
George, 1923-
BV4596.G38 B655 2002
242′.8 – dc21
                                                                2001007522

1   2   3   4   5   6   7   8   9   10   08   07   06   05   04   03   02

For Philip H. Schatz
alter ipse amicus

Contents

Foreword

Gay and lesbian Christians need to recognize themselves in liturgy. We don't need to invent liturgy from scratch, because so much of Christian liturgy is already of our making. We couldn't invent it from scratch, since the strongest liturgies are never merely invented. Still, as lesbians and gays trying to lead lives of faith in one or another of the Christian churches, we do need to recognize our lives within shared prayer.

William Storey helps us to recognize ourselves "as full members of the church." He has studied the liturgy as few believers do. He knows its old splendor, its varieties, its celestial harmony, and its tears. He can explain how a prayer-text came down to us or how a rite changed its shape over centuries. What is more important: he can make the most ancient rites vivid once again.

William Storey's prayer book reminds us that liturgical beauty goes together with theological truth. Indeed, the most truthful theology comes through liturgy. It gains in capacity for truth as it gains in power of expression. By contrast, too much church teaching is poor in expression and so in truth. Consider teaching on same-sex desire: it is often couched in the ugly, simplistic language of "official statements." We hear our lives — and not only our lives — caricatured as bureaucratic regulation. This prayer book shows why Christian teaching must speak more resonantly. Through the liturgy, theology begins to describe loves with some subtlety. It starts to inhabit fleshly bodies and to perform celebrations worthy of human experience. It responds to the God who comes toward us in our skin, speaking our language and celebrating our festivals.

Any prayer book is an invitation. This prayer book invites us, gently and wisely, to become more ourselves — not despite our loves, but because of them. "The Good News is especially for us."

MARK D. JORDAN
Asa Griggs Candler Professor of Religion,
Emory University

xi

Introduction

This is a prayer book designed for gay and lesbian Christians. It contains prayers collected from ancient, medieval, and modern sources that represent the solid and traditional attitudes toward God contained in the Holy Scriptures, the Apostles' Creed, the liturgies of various churches, and, above all, in the person of Jesus, the Word of God who speaks to us in and through his humanity.

Here "solid and traditional" describes prayers that embody and express the Good News in ways that ring true to the gospel as it has been understood by many generations of believing Christians. Their prayers express how millions of people feel about God, Christ, the church, and the daily challenges of human life. They are filled with faith, confidence, and hope in a God who never fails us even when we are at our lowest.

The prayers also breathe a spirit of love for God and for our fellow human beings. Despite our differences we are one body in Christ and share a responsibility for the health and nourishment of the whole body.

We live in the age of emerging consciousness of ourselves as lesbians and gay men. We belong to churches that used to persecute us and urge our destruction. Many of them still have serious doubts about our place in the church. However, there is also reason for hope, repentance, and change. New books appear almost daily that express more adequate views of homosexuals and their needs. Theologians are more ready to show that the old teaching about homosexuality is based on a series of misunderstandings of the Scriptures, of sexuality, and of other basic human needs. Even some of the "biased" official documents that have appeared recently are less prejudiced than earlier ones.

Attitudes are changing and we are changing. It is our task and privilege to boost our own self-respect and to present ourselves before God and our fellow believers as full members of the church. We shall win acceptance only to the degree that we are open about who we are. Nothing is more disconcerting to the ignorant and the prejudiced than gay people who live honestly, openly, and without apology.

When we pray, we do not need to hide who we really are or pretend to possess virtues that we don't actually have. We can be honest in speaking to God, who reads the heart and not just the lips. Our strong feelings will lead us to new decisions, help us work for change in ourselves and in our relationships, and resist the tendency we all have to become apathetic in the face of adversity.

This book contains a variety of prayers. There are prayers that express fear, doubt, and anger. There are also prayers for those who wonder if they are or even want to be members of churches that demean them. In other words, this prayer book contains prayers for the totally committed, the partially committed, the deeply troubled, and the alienated!

Anybody who would even consider using this prayer book is already on the road to faith — in some manner or form. But let's not get trapped by the idea that only *good* people pray. As we say so well in the Lord's Prayer: "Forgive us our sins as we forgive those who sin against us." If we can bring ourselves to forgive those who demean us, we shall find ourselves in the wonderful position of being the free recipient of total forgiveness. We are reminded of Jesus on the cross surrounded by the professionally religious people of his time and place, jeering and deriding him. Maybe we too will find ourselves able to join him in saying: "Father, forgive them, for they know not what they do." Or as the Virgin Mary put it in her canticle: "He has pulled down the mighty from their thrones and has lifted up the lowly." In the sight of many people, we may still be untouchables and sinners. In the sight of God, we are his beloved sons and daughters with a dignity all our own. The Good News is especially for us!

It is up to each person or group to select the prayers and rituals that can be prayed honestly from the heart. I suspect that many people will, for example, be able to start using the daily morning and evening prayers. But even in this case, "less is more." The main thing is not to race through a whole set of prayers but to pray slowly and carefully and for as long as we feel comfortable. Growth in prayer is a slow process that demands attention, devotion, and a certain amount of time each day. As St. Francis de Sales said: "Haste is the death of devotion."

Finally, this prayer book is a work of collaboration. Many gay and lesbian Christians have contributed their insights and prayers. I thank them all for their support and inspiration. The prayer book also tries to be ecumenical. Leaving aside the negative, hostile, and derogatory attitudes of our divided past, Christians may find it possible to use a prayer book that draws on many sources. In particular, it draws inspiration from the many new liturgical books that have been published recently. Whether they be Anglican, Lutheran, Methodist, Presbyterian, or Roman Catholic, they all share a basic attitude and approach to prayer — both communal and private — that can be said to be common. Furthermore, in this prayer book you will find passages from the Psalms and Hebrew Scriptures, readings and prayers from the New Testament and from later Christian poets, mystics, theologians, and writers of many eras. They all constitute a rich treasury of material. The intention is to provide a prayer book that can be used — in whole or in part — by a variety of Christians.

One

DAILY PRAYERS

The following prayers are often memorized and used daily. They can also be used when we feel under stress and don't know what words to use in our prayer.

◈ THE LORD'S PRAYER

At the request of his disciples, Jesus himself taught us how to pray. Even before John's Gospel was completed around the year 100, we were instructed to say the Lord's Prayer three times each day. Here is the modern version of it that is used in most Christian denominations:

Our Father in heaven,
hallowed be your name,
your kingdom come,
your will be done,
    on earth as in heaven.
Give us today our daily bread.
Forgive us our sins
    as we forgive those who sin against us.
Save us from the time of trial
    and deliver us from evil.
For the kingdom and the power and the glory
    are yours,
        now and for ever. Amen.

⬥ THE APOSTLES' CREED

In the second century, the church at Rome composed three questions addressed to those to be immersed in the baptismal pool:

Bishop: Do you believe in God the Father almighty,
                creator of heaven and earth?

Candidate: I do believe. [*immersion*]

Bishop: Do you believe in Jesus Christ,
                God's only Son, our Lord,
                who was born of the Virgin Mary,
                suffered, was crucified, and rose again?

Candidate: I do believe. [*immersion*]

Bishop: Do you believe in the Holy Spirit,
                in the holy catholic church,
                the communion of saints, the forgiveness of sins,
                and life everlasting?

Candidate: I do believe. [*immersion*]

At a later period these three questions were turned into a creed that came to be called the Apostles' Creed. It was not only a statement of basic Christian beliefs, but also an act of commitment to the Triune God revealed in Holy Scripture. Almost all Christians still use it to renew their baptismal promises to the Holy Trinity.

I believe in God, the Father almighty,
Creator of heaven and earth.

I believe in Jesus Christ, God's only Son, our Lord,
who was conceived by the Holy Spirit,
born of the Virgin Mary,
suffered under Pontius Pilate,
was crucified, died, and was buried;
he descended to the dead.
On the third day he rose again;
he ascended into heaven,
he is seated at the right hand of the Father,
and he will come to judge the living and the dead.

I believe in the Holy Spirit,
the holy catholic church,
the communion of saints,
the forgiveness of sins,
the resurrection of the body,
and the life everlasting. Amen.

◌ **THE DOXOLOGY**

Early Christians also composed hymns to glorify God,
and the doxology became a common form of praise:

Glory to the Father, and to the Son,
and to the Holy Spirit:
as it was in the beginning, is now,
and will be for ever. *Amen.*

Other Forms of the Doxology

Glory to God, Source of all being,
eternal Word, and Holy Spirit:
as it was in the beginning, is now,
and will be for ever. Amen.

> — *People's Companion to the Breviary* (Indianapolis:
> Carmelite Monastery, 1997), vol. 1, p. 1

Glory to God: Creator, Redeemer, and Sanctifier:
now and always and for ever and ever. Amen.

Glory to the holy and undivided Trinity,
now and always and for ever and ever. Amen.

To the Ruler of the ages, immortal invisible,
the only wise God,
be honor and glory, through Jesus Christ,
for ever and ever. Amen.

> — 1 Timothy 1:17; Romans 16:17

Two

MORNING AND
EVENING PRAYER

> Prayer is the key of morning and the bolt of evening.
> *Mahatma Gandhi*

Opening and closing the day with prayer is common to all religions but in a special way to the Semitic traditions of Judaism, Christianity, and Islam. If we desire to walk in the footsteps of Jesus as his disciples, fundamental to our spiritual life each day is morning and evening prayer.

These privileged times of prayer permit and encourage us to praise and thank God through Christ and the Holy Spirit at the beginning and close of each day. It is also an appropriate time for prayers of intercession for our needs, the needs of other Christians, and those of the whole world.

The Christian week was inherited and developed from Judaism and early Christianity. The Sabbath of the Old Law brought the week of work and prayer to a close and commemorated God's great work of creation. It was a day of peace and quiet dedicated to rest, prayer, and common worship. In New Testament times, the first day of the week, the Lord's Day, was designed to begin the week.

Before Holy Week developed as part of the extended liturgical year leading up to Easter, there was an earlier "holy week" that included the memorial of the passion and death of Christ on Fridays and that of the resurrection on Sundays. Furthermore, throughout this "holy week" two days, Wednesday and Friday, were devoted to prayer, fasting, and gifts or alms to the poor.

Although most churches no longer include these latter observances as part of the Christian week, they provide new meaning for those who serve the sick and dying with gifts of time, care, and money. The Christian week reminds us that the paschal mystery of Jesus' death and resurrection is central to the Christian message. Christians are called to die and rise with Christ each day through acts of self-sacrifice, service to others, and dedication to the poorest of the poor.

> Bless the Lord at all times,
> in the morning and in the evening.
> — *Daniel 3:71*

ᘒ THE LORD'S DAY: THE FIRST DAY OF THE WEEK

In English-speaking countries, Sunday is the usual name for the first day of the week, but in many Christian countries people refer to it as *Dominica, Dimanche, Domingo* ("the Lord's Day") or in Russian as *Voskresenie* ("the Day of the Resurrection").

Sunday has always been "a holy day of obligation" because the weekly gathering was considered essential to the very existence of the church. The church gathered each week to remember in Word and Sacrament the Risen Christ. In so doing, it became the visible Body of Christ. Stepping apart from that community of worship meant that a person was no longer a member of the Christian community:

> On the Lord's Day you should assemble and celebrate the Eucharist but first having confessed your transgressions, in order that your sacrifice may be untainted. No one who has had a quarrel with a fellow Christian should join your assembly until they have made up, so that your sacrifice may not be defiled. For this is what the Lord meant when he said: "At every place and time offer me a clean sacrifice for I am a great king, says the Lord, and my name is wonderful among the heathen." (Malachi 1:11, 14)
>
> > — *The Didache* (Teaching of the Apostles), section 14, Syria or Asia Minor, late 1st century, trans. Herbert A. Musurillo, S.J., *The Fathers of the Primitive Church* (New York: New American Library, 1966), p. 61

Morning and evening prayer on the Lord's Day are also an essential part of that weekly celebration. They portray the same central mysteries and help us to reflect and meditate on what they mean for our lives. Like all the daily devotions, Sunday morning and evening prayer has the following structure:

- opening verses with a hymn or poem,

- a psalm or canticle with a pause for reflection and a prayer,

- a brief lesson from Holy Scripture with a pause for meditation,

- appropriate verses after the reading,

- a canticle from the Scriptures,

- concluding prayers.

Although the following daily prayers will be used mostly by individuals, they are designed also for two or more people. Directions, or rubrics, in italics have been suggested to help groups pray together more easily. These rubrics appear only on the Sunday prayers but are meant to be implemented for daily use. A + in the text indicates that the sign of the cross may be made at this point. A tilde (~) introduces lines intended for group response.

ᘒ MORNING PRAYER ON THE LORD'S DAY

Leader: Blessed be God: Father, + Son, and Holy Spirit,

All: ~*Now and for ever. Amen.*

Hymn

The leader alternates the stanzas of the hymn with the group.

O come and let us worship Christ!
All people bow before him
Who from the dead a Victor rose:
Sing praises and adore him.

The stone was sealed upon the tomb,
And soldiers guard were keeping,
Where in the cold embrace of death
The Christ of God was sleeping.

The morning star shone in the east,
The hills with light were glowing;
The Christ arose, upon the world
His light and life bestowing.

Wherefore from highest heaven the hosts
Their songs of victory blending,
Give glory to the mighty Lord,
And sing his reign unending. Amen.

> — Text: Trans. John Brownlie (1857–1925),
> *Hymns of the Greek Church* (London, 1900)

Canticle of Isaiah   *Isaiah 61:1–3, 10–11*

All recite the antiphon in unison.

Antiphon: The Lord has risen for his people, alleluia!

The leader alternates the stanzas of the canticle with the group.

The spirit of the Lord is upon me,
because the Lord has anointed me;
he has sent me to bring good news to the oppressed,
to bind up the brokenhearted,
to proclaim liberty to the captives,
and release to the prisoners;
to proclaim the year of the Lord's favor,
and the day of vengeance of our God;

to comfort all who mourn;
to provide for those who mourn in Zion —
to give them a garland instead of ashes,
the oil of gladness instead of mourning,
the mantle of praise instead of a faint spirit.
They will be called oaks of righteousness,
the planting of the Lord, to display his glory.

I will greatly rejoice in the Lord,
my whole being shall exult in my God;
for he has clothed me with the garments of salvation,
he has covered me with the robe of righteousness,
as a bridegroom decks himself with a garland,
as a bride adorns herself with her jewels.

For as earth brings forth its shoots,
and as a garden causes what is sown in it to spring up,
so the Lord God will cause righteousness and praise
to spring up before all the nations.

All repeat the antiphon in unison.

Antiphon: The Lord has risen for his people, alleluia!

Prayer

> *Leader:* Let us pray (*pause for quiet prayer*)
>
>> Lord Jesus Christ, our risen Savior,
>> during your life on earth
>> you brought good news to the oppressed,
>> comforted the poor and afflicted,
>> and clothed us with the garments of salvation.
>> Be now our present Savior,
>> and help us to die daily to all sin,
>> that we may live for ever
>> in the joy of your risen life;
>> we ask it for your own name's sake.
>
> *All:* ~Amen.

Reading   THE NEW COVENANT   *Hebrews 12:22–24, 28*

You have come to Mount Zion and to the city of the living God, the
heavenly Jerusalem, and to innumerable angels in festal gathering,
and to the assembly of the firstborn who are enrolled in heaven,
and to God the judge of all, and to the spirits of the righteous made
perfect, and to Jesus the mediator of the new covenant, and to the
sprinkled blood that speaks a better word than the blood of Abel.
Therefore since we are receiving a kingdom that cannot be shaken,
let us give thanks, by which we offer to God an acceptable worship
with reverence and awe.

Pause for meditation

Response

> *Leader:* Your holy cross, O Lord, alleluia!
>
> *All:* ~Is the Tree of life, alleluia!

The Song of the Church   *Te Deum Laudamus*

The leader alternates the stanzas with the group.

We praise you, O God,
we acclaim you as Lord;
all creation worships you,
the Father everlasting.

To you all angels, all the powers of heaven,
the Cherubim and Seraphim, sing in endless praise:
    Holy, holy, holy Lord, God of power and might,
    heaven and earth are full of your glory.

The glorious company of apostles praise you.
The noble fellowship of prophets praise you.
The white-robed army of martyrs praise you.

Throughout the world the holy church acclaims you:
    Father, of majesty unbounded,
    your true and only Son, worthy of all praise,
    and the Holy Spirit, advocate and guide.

You, Christ, are the king of glory,
the eternal Son of the Father.
When you took our flesh to set us free
you humbly chose the Virgin's womb.

You overcame the sting of death,
and opened the kingdom of heaven to all believers.
You are seated at God's right hand in glory.
We believe that you will come to be our judge.

Come then, Lord, and help your people,
bought with the price of your own blood,
and bring us with your saints
to glory everlasting.

Prayer

    Leader: God of peace,
           by the blood of the eternal covenant,
           you brought back from the dead
           the great Shepherd of the sheep,
           Jesus our Lord.

> Make us ready to do your will
> by performing every kind of good deed
> that is pleasing in your sight,
> through Jesus Christ,
> to whom be glory for ever and ever.

All: ~*Amen.*

Blessing

Leader: May he who rose from the dead,
Christ our true God, + bless us and keep us.

All: ~ *Amen.*

ᨒ EVENING PRAYER ON THE LORD'S DAY

Leader: Christ + is risen, alleluia!

All: ~*He is risen, indeed, alleluia!*

Hymn

The leader alternates the stanzas with the group.

O radiant Light, O Sun divine
Of God the Father's deathless face,
O Image of the light sublime
That fills the heavenly dwelling place:

O Son of God, the source of life,
Praise is your due by night and day;
Our happy lips must raise the strain
Of your esteemed and splendid name.

Lord Jesus Christ, as daylight fades,
As shine the lights of eventide,
We praise the Father with the Son,
The Spirit blest and with them one. Amen.

— Text: *Phos hilaron,* Greek, 2nd–3rd century,
trans. William G. Storey

Canticle of Isaiah   *Isaiah 60:1–3, 18–20*

All recite the antiphon in unison.

Antiphon: The Lord will be your everlasting light, alleluia!

The leader alternates the stanzas of the canticle with the group.

Arise, shine; for your light has come,
and the glory of the Lord has risen upon you.
For darkness shall cover the earth,
and thick darkness the peoples;
but the Lord will arise upon you,
and his glory will appear over you.
Nations shall come to your light,
and kings to the brightness of your dawn.

Violence shall no more be heard in your land,
devastation or destruction within your borders;
you shall call your walls Salvation,
and your gates Praise.

The sun shall no longer be your light by day,
nor for brightness shall the moon give light to you by night;
but the Lord will be your everlasting light,
and your God will be your glory.

Your sun shall no more go down,
or your moon withdraw itself;
for the Lord will be your everlasting light,
and your days of mourning shall be ended.

All repeat the antiphon in unison.

Antiphon: The Lord will be your everlasting light, alleluia!

Prayer

Leader: Let us pray (*pause for quiet prayer*)

Father of glory,
you raised Jesus Christ from the dead
and made him sit at your right hand.
Rescue us from our sins,
bring us to new life in him,

raise us up with him,
and give us a place with him in heaven,
through the same Christ our Lord.

All: ~*Amen.*

Reading   THE RESURRECTION   *1 Corinthians 15:1–8*

Now I would remind you, brothers and sisters, of the good news
that I proclaimed to you...through which you are being saved.
...For I handed on to you as of first importance what I in turn
had received: that Christ died for ours sins in accordance with the
scriptures, and that he was buried, and that he was raised on the
third day in accordance with the scriptures, and that he appeared
to Cephas, then to the twelve. Then he appeared to more than
five hundred bothers and sisters, most of whom are still alive,
though some have died. Then he appeared to James, then to all
the apostles. Last of all, as to one untimely born, he appeared
also to me.

Pause for meditation

Response

Leader: From Eden's tree came death, alleluia!

All: ~*From Calvary's cross came life, alleluia!*

Canticle of the Virgin Mary   *Luke 1:46–55*

All recite the antiphon in unison.

Antiphon: We are Easter people and alleluia is our song!

The leader alternates the stanzas of the canticle with the group.

My soul + proclaims the greatness of the Lord,
my spirit rejoices in God my Savior,
for you, Lord, have looked with favor on your lowly servant.

From this day all generations will call me blessed:
you, the Almighty, have done great things for me
and holy is your name.
You have mercy on those who fear you,
from generation to generation.

You have shown strength with your arm
and scattered the proud in their conceit,
casting down the mighty from their thrones
and lifting up the lowly.
You have filled the hungry with good things
and sent the rich away empty.

You have come to the aid of your servant Israel,
to remember the promise of mercy,
the promise made to our forebears,
to Abraham and his children for ever.

Glory to God, Abba, our dear Father,
the Word divine, and the Holy Spirit,
our advocate and guide:

now and always and for ever and ever. Amen.

All repeat the antiphon in unison.

Antiphon: We are Easter people and alleluia is our song!

Litany

    Leader: Lord Jesus, living stone,
            rejected by your own people, but chosen by God,

      All: ~*Lord, hear our prayer.*

         Lord Jesus, put to death in the flesh,
         raised to life in the Spirit,
         ~*Lord, hear our prayer.*

         Lord Jesus, Lamb of God, without spot or stain,
         ~*Lord, hear our prayer.*

         Lord Jesus, shepherd and guardian of our souls,
         ~*Lord, hear our prayer.*

         Lord Jesus, seated at the Father's right hand in glory,
         ~*Lord, hear our prayer.*

         Lord Jesus, who will come again in glory
         to judge the living and the dead,
         ~*Lord, hear our prayer.*

Lord Jesus, whose kingdom shall have no end.
~*Lord, hear our prayer.*

Spontaneous prayers of intercession

Prayer

Leader: Only begotten Son and eternal Word of God,
for us and for our salvation,
you took flesh of the Virgin Mary
and came to live among us as a man.
For our sake you were crucified,
mastered death and the grave,
and rose again on the third day.
Forgive us our sins
and sanctify us to your service,
for you are the joy of those who love you,
O Savior of the world,
living and reigning with the Father and the Holy Spirit,
now and for ever.

All: ~*Amen.*

Blessing

Leader: May the Lord bless us and keep us;
may the Lord make his face shine on us
and be gracious to us;
may the Lord + grant us peace.

All: ~*Amen.*

⊗ MONDAY MORNING PRAYER

Leader: Our help + is in the name of the Lord,

All: ~*Who made heaven and earth.*

Hymn

I sing as I arise today!
I call upon the Father's might:
The will of God to be my guide,
The eye of God to be my sight.

God to be my speech,
The hand of God to be my stay,
The shield of God to be my strength,
The path of God to be my way.

— Text: Ascribed to St. Patrick (372–466); trans. anon.

Psalm 100   PRAISE AND THANKSGIVING

Antiphon: Worship the Lord in the beauty of holiness.

Make a joyful noise to the Lord, all you lands!
serve the Lord with gladness!
Come into God's presence with singing!

Know that the Lord, who made us, is God.
We are the Lord's;
we are the people of God,
the sheep of God's pasture.

Enter God's gates with thanksgiving,
and God's courts with praise!
Give thanks and bless God's name!

For the Lord is good;
God's steadfast love endures for ever,
God's faithfulness to all generations.

Antiphon: Worship the Lord in the beauty of holiness.

Prayer

Leader: Let us pray (*pause for quiet prayer*)

Lord our God,
it is our duty and our joy
to praise and thank you
today and every day.
You are our Creator and our Savior,
faithful from age to age,
and we bless your holy name,
through Christ Jesus our Lord.

All: ~*Amen.*

Reading   MY YOKE IS EASY   *Matthew 11:28–30*

Jesus says: "Come to me, all you that are weary and are carrying heavy burdens, and I will give you rest. Take my yoke upon you, and learn from me; for I am gentle and humble in heart, and you will find rest for your souls. For my yoke is easy, and my burden is light."

Pause for meditation

Response

   Leader: Send forth your light and your truth;

      All: ~*Let these be my guide.*

Canticle of Daniel   *Daniel 3:52–57*

Antiphon: Bless the Lord, sing to God's glory!

Blest are you, O Lord, God of our ancestors,
praised and glorified above all for ever!
Blest your glorious and holy name,
praised and glorified above all for ever!

Blest are you in your temple of glory,
praised and glorified above all for ever!
Blest are you on your cherubim throne,
praised and lifted above all for ever!

Blest are you enthroned in majesty,
praised and glorified above all for ever!
Blest are you in the starry vault of heaven,
praised and glorified above all for ever!

Bless the Lord, sing to God's glory,
all things fashioned by God's mighty hand.

Glory to God: Creator, Redeemer, and Sanctifier:

now and always, and for ever and ever. Amen.

Antiphon: Bless the Lord, sing to God's glory!

Prayer

Leader: Lord God almighty,
           you are the beginning and the end,
           the first and the last.
           Direct our hearts and bodies
           in the love of God and the patience of Christ;
           bless us, defend us from all evil,
           and bring us in safety to life everlasting;
           through Jesus Christ our Lord.

All: ~*Amen.*

Blessing

Leader: May the Word made flesh,
           full of grace and truth,
           + bless us and keep us.

All: ~*Amen.*

⚶ MONDAY EVENING PRAYER

Leader: Light and peace + in Jesus Christ our Lord.

All: ~*Thanks be to God.*

Hymn

Lord Jesus Christ, abide with us,
Now that the sun has run its course;
Let hope not be obscured by night
But may faith's darkness be as light.

Lord Jesus Christ, grant us your peace,
And when the trials of earth shall cease;
Grant us the morning light of grace,
The radiant splendor of your face.

Immortal, Holy, Threefold Light,
Yours be the kingdom, power, and might;
All glory be eternally
To you, life-giving Trinity! Amen.

> — Text: *Mane nobiscum, Domine,* para.
> © St. Joseph's Abbey, Spencer, Mass.

Psalm 121   GOD IS ALWAYS WAKEFUL

Antiphon: Watch and pray and you will not fall into temptation.

I lift up my eyes to the hills —
from where does my help come?
My help comes from the Lord,
who made heaven and earth.

The Lord will not let your foot be moved,
the Lord who keeps you will not slumber.
The One who keeps Israel
will neither slumber nor sleep.

The Lord is your keeper;
the Lord is your shade
on your right hand.
The sun shall not strike you by day,
nor the moon by night.

The Lord will keep you from all evil,
and will keep your life.
The Lord will keep your going out
and your coming in
from this time forth and for evermore.

Antiphon: Watch and pray and you will not fall into temptation.

Prayer

> *Leader:* Let us pray (*pause for quiet prayer*)
>
> > God our protector,
> > unsleeping guardian of your people,
> > defend us by day and by night
> > from the obstacles which the world,
> > the flesh, and the devil put in our path.
> > We ask this through Christ our Lord.
>
> *All:* ~Amen.

Reading   A LAMP   *Matthew 5:14–16*

You are the light of the world. A city built on a hill cannot be hid.
No one after lighting a lamp puts it under the bushel basket, but
on the lampstand, and it gives light to all in the house. In the same

way, let your light shine before others, so that they may see your
good works and give glory to your Father in heaven.

Pause for meditation

Response

> *Leader:* Praise the Lord's name
>
> *All:* ~*From sunrise to sunset.*

Canticle of Revelation   *Revelation 4:11; 5:9–10, 12*

Antiphon: Jesus is the Lamb of God
           who takes away the sins of the world.

You are worthy, our Lord and God,
to receive glory and honor and power,
for you created all things,
and by your will they existed
and were created.

You are worthy to take the scroll
and to open its seals,
for you were slaughtered
and by your blood you ransomed for God
saints from every tribe and language
and people and nation;
you have made them to be a kingdom
and priests serving our God.

Worthy is the Lamb that was slaughtered
to receive power and wealth
and wisdom and might
and honor and glory and blessing!

Glory to the Father, and to the Son,
and to the Holy Spirit:

as it was in the beginning, is now,
and will be for ever. Amen.

Antiphon: Jesus is the Lamb of God
           who takes away the sins of the world.

Litany

Leader: Let us complete our evening prayer to the Lord.

All: ~*Lord, have mercy.*

For an angel of peace to guide and guard
our souls and bodies,
let us pray to the Lord.
~*Lord, have mercy.*

For the good earth which God has given us
and for the wisdom and will to conserve it,
let us pray to the Lord.
~*Lord, have mercy.*

For those who travel by land, sea, or air,
let us pray to the Lord.
~*Lord, have mercy.*

For the aged and infirm, for widows and orphans,
and for the sick and suffering,
let us pray to the Lord.
~*Lord, have mercy.*

For the poor and oppressed,
the unemployed and the homeless,
for prisoners and the persecuted,
and for all who care for them,
let us pray to the Lord.
~*Lord, have mercy.*

For all who have died in the peace of Christ,
especially *N*_____
let us pray to the Lord.
~*Lord, have mercy.*

For the forgiveness of all our sins and offenses,
let us pray to the Lord.
~*Lord, have mercy.*

For a peaceful death without stain or pain,
let us pray to the Lord.
~*Lord, have mercy.*

Help, save, pity, and defend us, O Lord, by your grace.

Pause for special intentions.

Leader: Rejoicing in the communion of the Holy Spirit,
and of all the saints, let us commend ourselves,
one another, and our whole life to Christ our Lord.

All: ~*To you, O Lord.*

Prayer

Leader: Heavenly Father,
hear the prayers of your faithful people
who put their trust in your mercy.
Be our comforter in time of need,
be the strength of the sick and sorrowful,
and give rest to our beloved dead.
We ask this through Christ our Lord.

All: ~*Amen.*

Blessing

Leader: May the blessing of almighty God,
who is gracious and loves the human race,
+ descend upon us and remain with us for ever.

All: ~*Amen.*

◌ TUESDAY MORNING PRAYER

Leader: O Lord, + open my lips,

All: ~*And my mouth will proclaim your praise.*

Hymn

Father of mercies, heaven's eternal Dayspring,
Maker of all things, shine on your creation,
visit your children, born to share your glory,
heirs of your Kingdom.

Son of the Father, splendor born of splendor,
star of the morning, sun that knows no setting,

come now in blessing, God's true Word and Wisdom,
Dawn of salvation.

Spirit of Jesus, fire of love descending,
warmth of our spirit, light when all is darkness,
strength in our weakness, joy in every sorrow,
be with us always.

> — James Quinn, S.J., *Praise for All Seasons*
> (Kingston, N.Y.: Selah Publishing Co., 1994), p. 53.

Psalm 63   LONGING FOR GOD

Antiphon: My God, for you I long from break of day.

O God, you are my God,
I seek you, I thirst for you;
my flesh faints for you,
as in a dry and weary land where no water is.
So I have looked upon you in the sanctuary,
beholding your power and glory.

Because your steadfast love is better than life,
my lips will praise you.
So I will bless you as long as I live;
I will lift up my hands and call on your name.

My soul is feasted as with marrow and fat,
and my mouth praises you with joyful lips,
when I think of you upon my bed,
and meditate on you in the watches of the night.

For you have been my help,
and in the shadow of your wings I sing for joy.
My soul clings to you;
your right hand upholds me.

Antiphon: My God, for you I long from break of day.

Prayer

> *Leader:* Let us pray (*pause for quiet prayer*)
>
>   Author of undying light,
>   your love is better than life
>   and our souls are restless

until they rest in you.
May our lips praise you,
and our lives glorify you,
through Jesus our Lord and Savior.

All: ~*Amen.*

Reading   HOW TO PRAY   *Matthew 6:5–6*

Whenever you pray, do not be like the hypocrites; for they love to
stand and pray in the synagogues and at the street corners, so that
they may be seen by others. Truly I tell you, they have received
their reward. But whenever you pray, go into your room and shut
the door and pray to your Father who is in secret; and your Father
who sees in secret will reward you.

Pause for meditation

Response

Leader: I pray to you, Lord,

All: ~*My prayer rises like the sun.*

Canticle of Daniel   DIVINE PRAISE   *Daniel 3:56–73*

Antiphon: Creation eagerly awaits
the full revelation of God in Christ.

Bless the Lord, sing to God's glory,
all things fashioned by God's mighty hand;
Praise God's strength, sing to God's name,
in the present age and in eternity.

Praise the Lord, all you holy angels,
who assist with reverence at God's holy throne.
Let the blue skies bless the Lord,
and all the heavenly sphere embraces.

Bless the Lord, all you waters,
which reside above the heavens;
All the great powers of the Lord,
sing God's praises for ever.

Let the sun and moon bless the Lord,
they whose rays put to flight the darkness.

Let the great and brilliant stars
give their light to praise God's greatness.

Bless the Lord, all heavenly dew,
bless the Lord, every drop of moisture.
Bless the Lord, all mighty winds,
you ministers of God's majesty.

Bless the Lord, all fire and heat,
which dry the earth in summer time.
Bless the Lord, all icy blasts,
which bring snow and ice in winter.

Bless the Lord, all mists and frosts,
which crown the peaks of mountains.
Let each day and night of the year
and changing seasons bless the Lord.

Bless the Lord, at all times,
both in the morning and in the evening.
And may the dark clouds bless the Lord,
through the terror of the lightning.

Let us bless the Father, the Son, and the Holy Spirit,
one holy and undivided Trinity;
Blessed are you, Lord, in the highest heavens,
you who reign supreme over all creation.

Antiphon: Creation eagerly awaits
the full revelation of God in Christ.

Prayer

Leader: Creator of heaven and earth,
you fashioned the powers of human reasoning
and of rational speech.
Accept our hymns of praise
that we offer in union with all creation,
for all the powers of heaven and earth
acclaim and exalt you, now and for ever.

All: ~*Amen.*

Blessing

Leader: May the Creator God,
who fashions all things by his mighty hand,
+ bless us and keep us.

All: ~*Amen.*

ᏧᎳ TUESDAY EVENING PRAYER

Leader: Jesus Christ + is the light of the world,

All: ~*A light no darkness can extinguish.*

Hymn

The setting sun now dies away,
And darkness comes at close of day;
Your radiant hope, O Lord, impart
To every mind and every heart.

We praise your name with joy this night;
O watch and guide us till the light
That we may rest within your grace
And know the calm that is your peace.

To God the Father, God the Son,
And Holy Spirit, Three in One,
Trinity blest, whom we adore,
Be praise and glory evermore. Amen.

> — Text: *Iam sol recedit igneus,* trans. Geoffrey Laycock, based
> on *The Primer,* 1706, © Faber Music Ltd.; adapted by Ralph
> Wright, O.S.B., © GIA Publications, Inc.

Psalm 122   GOD'S CITY, GOD'S HOUSE, GOD'S JOY

Antiphon: I will go to the altar of God,
the God of my joy.

I was glad when they said to me,
"Let us go to the house of the Lord!"
Our feet were standing
within your gates, O Jerusalem!

Jerusalem is built as a city
bound tightly together,

to which the tribes go up,
the tribes of the Lord,
to give thanks to the name of the Lord,
as was decreed for Israel.

Thrones for judgment were set up there,
the thrones of the house of David.
Pray for the peace of Jerusalem;
"May they prosper who love you!
Peace be within your walls,
and security within your towers!"

For the sake of my relatives and friends,
I will say, "Peace be within you!"
For the sake of the house of the Lord our God,
I will seek your good.

Antiphon: I will go to the altar of God,
              the God of my joy.

Prayer

Leader: Let us pray (*pause for quiet prayer*)

God of your chosen people,
you are the theme of our prayer
as we honor your holy name.
Grant peace, happiness, and safety
to our family and friends
who gather about your altar.
We ask this through Christ our Lord.

All: ~*Amen.*

Reading   INTERCESSORY PRAYER   *1 Timothy 2:1–4*

I urge that supplications, prayers, intercessions, and thanksgiving
be made for everyone, for kings and all who are in high positions,
so that we may lead a quiet and peaceable life in all godliness and
dignity. This is right and is acceptable in the sight of God our Savior,
who desires everyone to be saved and to come to the knowledge of
the truth.

Pause for meditation

Response

> *Leader:* Your word is a lamp for my feet
>
> *All:* ~*And a light for my path.*

Canticle of Revelation   *Revelation 15:3–4*

Antiphon: Glory to God in the highest!

Great and amazing are your deeds,
Lord God the Almighty!
Just and true are your ways,
King of the nations!

Lord, who will not fear
and glorify your name?
For you alone are holy.

All nations will come
and worship before you,
for your judgments have been revealed.

Glory to God: Creator, Redeemer, and Sanctifier:

now and always, and for ever and ever. Amen.

Antiphon: Glory to God in the highest!

Litany

> *Leader:* Lord Jesus Christ, God from God and light from light,
>
> *All:* ~*Be our light and our salvation.*
>
> Lord Jesus Christ, source of life and holiness,
> ~*Be our light and our salvation.*
>
> Lord Jesus Christ, hope of the sick and the poor,
> ~*Be our light and our salvation.*
>
> Lord Jesus Christ, mighty defender of the sick
> and the dying,
> ~*Be our light and our salvation.*
>
> Lord Jesus Christ, light and peace of the faithful dead,
> ~*Be our light and our salvation.*
>
> *Spontaneous prayers of intercession*

Prayer

> *Leader:* Lord our God,
> whose power is beyond all words to describe,
> whose glory is without measure,
> whose mercy is without limits,
> and whose love for us is beyond all telling:
> In your kindness, grant to us
> and to all those praying with us,
> the riches of your compassion and mercy;
> for the sake of Jesus, our Savior and Lord.

> *All:* ~*Amen.*

Blessing

> *Leader:* May Christ, the light and love of the world,
> + bless us and keep us.

> *All:* ~*Amen.*

⊙ WEDNESDAY MORNING PRAYER

> *Leader:* Holy is God, + holy and strong, holy and living for ever.

> *All:* ~*Lord, have mercy on us.*

Hymn

The day is filled with splendor
When God brings light from light,
And all renewed creation
Rejoices in his sight.

The Father gives his children
The wonder of the world
In which his power and glory
Like banners are unfurled.

With every living creature,
Awaking with the day,
We turn to God our Father,
Lift up our hearts and pray.

O Father, Son, and Spirit,
Your grace and mercy send,
That we may live to praise you
Today and to the end. Amen.

> — Text: James Socias, *Handbook of Prayers*
> (Princeton, N.J.: Scepter Publishers, 1997), p. 49

Psalm 67   A CALL TO PRAISE

Antiphon: Let the peoples praise you, O God,
            let all the peoples praise you!

O God, be gracious to us and bless us
and make your face to shine upon us,
that your way may be known upon earth,
your saving power among all nations.

Let the peoples praise you, O God,
let all the peoples praise you!

Let the nations be glad, and sing for joy,
for you judge the peoples with equity
and guide the nations upon earth.

Let the peoples praise you, O God,
let all the peoples praise you!

The earth has yielded its increase;
God, our God, has blessed us.
May God bless us;
let all the ends of the earth fear God!

Antiphon: Let the peoples praise you, O God,
            let all the peoples praise you!

Prayer

Leader: Let us pray (*pause for quiet prayer*)

          Christ our Lord,
          you are both our way to heaven
          and our heavenly home itself.
          You are our Savior here and now;

      be our joy and our reward
      through all eternity.
      You live and reign from age to age.

   All: *~Amen.*

Reading   GOD AND WEALTH   *Matthew 6:19–21, 24*

Do not store up for yourselves treasures on earth, where moth and rust consume and where thieves break in and steal; but store up for yourselves treasures in heaven, where neither moth nor rust consume and where thieves do not break in and steal. For where your treasure is, there your heart will be also. No one can serve two masters; for a slave will either hate the one and love the other, or be devoted to the one and despise the other. You cannot serve God and wealth.

Pause for meditation

Response

   Leader: Shine your love on us each dawn,

      All: *~And gladden all our days.*

Canticle of Daniel   DIVINE PRAISE   *Daniel 3:74–87*

Antiphon: Creation shares the glorious freedom
             of the children of God.

Bless the Lord, sing to God's glory,
all things fashioned by God's mighty hand.
Praise God's strength, sing to God's name,
in the present age and in eternity.

Let the earth and all that is in it
praise the greatness of the Lord.
Let humans do all within their power
to extol the glory of God's name.

Let the towering mountains bless the Lord,
with the forests and the lowly hills.
Let flowers and plants bless the Lord,
every growing thing earth yields.

Bless the Lord, all flowing fountains,
which spring from far below the earth.

Bless the Lord, seas and rivers,
whose waters carry our laden ships.

Bless the Lord, fish and sea monsters,
all creatures living in the waters.
Bless the Lord, all you winged creatures,
who fly the heavens majestically.

Bless the Lord, all animals,
both the wild and the tame.
Bless the Lord, all you human creatures,
and praise God's goodness eternally.

Let us bless the Father, the Son, and the Holy Spirit,
one holy and undivided Trinity;
Blessed are you, Lord, in the highest heavens,
you who reign supreme over all creation.

Antiphon: Creation shares the glorious freedom
of the children of God.

Prayer

Leader: Holy and immortal God,
dwelling among the saints,
the seraphim praise you,
the cherubim sing your glory,
and all the powers of heaven and earth
fall down in adoration before you.
Allow us, sinful as we are,
to stand before your holy altar
and to offer you the worship you deserve,
through the merits of Christ our Savior,
who lives and reigns with you and the Holy Spirit,
now and for ever.

All: ~Amen.

Blessing

Leader: May grace and peace be ours in full measure
from the Father, + the Son, and the Holy Spirit,
now and for ever.

All: ~Amen.

ᓂ **WEDNESDAY EVENING PRAYER**

Leader: Our help + is the Lord,

All: ~*Creator of earth and sky.*

Hymn

Now from the altar of my heart
Let incense smoke arise;
Assist me, Lord, to offer up
My evening sacrifice.

Awake, my love; awake, my joy;
Awake, my heart and tongue!
Sleep not: when mercies loudly call,
Break forth into a song.

This day God was my sun and shield,
My keeper and my guide;
His care was on my frailty shown,
His mercies multiplied.

New time, new favor, and new joys
Do a new song require;
Till I shall praise you as I would,
Accept my heart's desire.

> — Text: John Mason (ca. 1645–1694), *The Hymn Book of the Anglican Church of Canada* (Toronto, 1971), #367, alt.

Psalm 126   A DREAM COME TRUE

Antiphon: God works wonders for his chosen ones.

When the Lord restored the fortunes of Zion,
we were like those who dream.
Then our mouth was filled with laughter,
and our tongue with shouts of joy;
then it was said among the nations,
"The Lord has done great things for them."

The Lord has done great things for us,
and we are glad.
Restore our fortunes, O Lord,
like the watercourses in the Negeb!

May those who sow in tears
reap with shouts of joy!
Those who go out weeping,
bearing the seeds for sowing,
shall come home with shouts of joy,
carrying their sheaves.

Antiphon: God works wonders for his chosen ones.

Prayer

> *Leader:* Let us pray (*pause for quiet prayer*)
>
> > God of loving kindness,
> > a church that loves justice
> > is the admiration of others
> > and the joy of its members.
> > Bring us back to the fullness of the Gospel
> > and make us laugh with shouts of joy
> > as we admire your wonders.
> > We ask this through Christ our Lord.
>
> *All:* ~Amen.

Reading   ALL ARE ONE IN CHRIST   *Galatians 3:25–29*

Now that faith has come, we are no longer subject to a disciplinar-
ian, for in Christ Jesus you are all children of God through faith. As
many of you as were baptized into Christ have clothed yourselves
with Christ. There is no longer Jew or Greek, there is no longer
slave or free, there is no longer male or female, [there is no longer
black or white, there is no longer gay or straight]; for all of you
are one in Christ Jesus. And if you belong to Christ, then you are
Abraham's offspring, heirs according to the promise.

Pause for meditation

Response

> *Leader:* At night lift up your hands in the holy place
>
> > *All:* ~And bless the Lord.

Canticle of Simeon

Luke 2:29–32

Antiphon: Light for the nations, glory for Israel!

Now, Lord, + let your servant go in peace;
your word has been fulfilled.

My own eyes have seen the salvation
which you have prepared in the sight of every people,

a light to reveal you to the nations
and the glory of your people Israel.

Glory to God, Source of all being,
eternal Word, and Holy Spirit,

as it was in the beginning, is now,
and will be for ever. Amen.

Antiphon: Light for the nations, glory for Israel!

Litany

Leader: Lord, have mercy.

All: *~Christ, have mercy. Lord, have mercy.*

Our Father in heaven,
~hallowed be your name,
your kingdom come,
your will be done,
on earth as in heaven.
Give us today our daily bread.
Forgive us our sins
as we forgive those who sin against us.
Save us from the time of trial
and deliver us from evil.
For the kingdom and the power and the glory are yours,
now and for ever. Amen.

Save your people, Lord, and bless your inheritance;
~Govern and uphold them, now and always.

Day by day we bless you;
~We praise your name for ever.

Lord, keep us from all sin tonight;
~Have mercy on us, Lord, have mercy.

Lord, show us your love and mercy
~For we put our trust in you.

In you, Lord, is our hope.
~And we shall never hope in vain.

— "Evening Prayer," *Book of Common Prayer* 1979, p. 98

Spontaneous prayers of intercession

Prayer

Leader: O God, the author of peace
and lover of concord,
to know you is eternal life
and to serve you is perfect freedom:
Defend us against all the assaults of our enemies,
visible and invisible,
that trusting in your help
we may not fear the power of any adversary;
through the might of Jesus Christ our Lord.

All: *~Amen.*

Blessing

Leader: May the peace of God,
which passes all understanding,
+ guard our hearts and our minds
in Christ Jesus our Lord.

All: *~Amen.*

⚘ THURSDAY MORNING PRAYER

Leader: Blessed + be the name of the Lord,

All: *~Now and for ever. Amen.*

Hymn

From all that dwell beneath the skies
Let the Creator's praise arise:

Let the Redeemer's name be sung
Through every land in every tongue.

Eternal are your mercies, Lord:
Eternal truth attends your word;
Your praise shall sound from shore to shore,
Till suns shall rise and set no more.

— Text: Isaac Watts (1674–1748) based on *Psalm 117*, alt.

Psalm 138   GOD GIVES STRENGTH AND PROTECTION

Antiphon: You have exalted your name
            and your word above everything.

I give you thanks, O Lord, with all my heart;
before the gods I sing your praise;
I bow down toward your holy temple
and give thanks to your name
for your steadfast love and faithfulness;
for you have exalted your name
and your word above everything.

On the day I called, you answered me,
you strengthened my life.
All the rulers of the earth shall praise you, O Lord,
for they have heard the words of your mouth.
They shall sing the ways of the Lord,
for great is the glory of the Lord.

For the Lord is high, but regards the lowly;
yet knows the conceited from afar.
Though I walk in the midst of trouble,
you preserve my life;
you stretch out your hand
against the wrath of my enemies
and your right hand delivers me.

O Lord, fulfill your promise for me;
may your steadfast love endure for ever.
Do not forsake the work of your hands.

Antiphon: You have exalted your name
            and your word above everything.

Prayer

Leader: Let us pray (*pause for quiet prayer*)

> Great is your glory, Lord,
> and your care for the poor and lowly.
> Reach out your hand to save us
> in time of trial and temptation
> and do not abandon what your hands have made.
> We make our prayer in Jesus' name.

All: ~*Amen.*

Reading   PRAYER AND SONG   *Colossians 3:15–17*

Let the peace of Christ rule in your hearts, to which indeed you
were called in the one body. And be thankful. Let the word of
Christ dwell in you richly; teach and admonish one another in all
wisdom; and with gratitude in your hearts sing psalms, hymns,
and spiritual songs to God. And whatever you do, in word or deed,
do everything in the name of the Lord Jesus, giving thanks to God
the Father through him.

Pause for meditation

Response

Leader: The Lord is my light and my salvation,

All: ~*Whom shall I fear?*

Canticle of Daniel   DIVINE PRAISES   *Daniel 3:82–88*

Antiphon: Praise the holy name,
this name beyond all names.

Bless the Lord, sing to his glory,
all things fashioned by God's mighty hand;
Praise God's strength, sing to God's name,
in the present age and in eternity.

O Israel, bless your God continually,
for ever and ever praise God's greatness.
Bless the Lord, all you his saints;
praise God's goodness eternally.

Bless the Lord, all you his priests;
bless God faithfully, all you his servants.
Bless the Lord, all you holy souls;
you who are humble and love the Lord.

Let everyone sing to God's glory and praise,
from the present moment until eternity.

Let us bless the Father, the Son, and the Holy Spirit,
one holy and undivided Trinity.
Blessed are you, Lord, in the highest heavens,
you who reign supreme over all creation.

Antiphon: Praise the holy name,
this name beyond all names.

Prayer

Leader: Let us pray (*pause for quiet prayer*)

Almighty God and Father,
all creation speaks eloquently
of your wonderful works.
Let your glory shine forth in us
that our human life may praise you,
in union with the whole company of heaven;
through Jesus Christ our Lord.

All: ~*Amen.*

Blessing

Leader: May the Lord bless + us,
and preserve us from all evil,
and bring us to everlasting life.

All: ~*Amen.*

❦ THURSDAY EVENING PRAYER

> *Leader:* I am the light + of the world, says the Lord;
>
> *All:* ~*Whoever follows me will not walk in darkness.*

Hymn

O Lord, Creator of all things,
The source of day and night,
You fashioned first of all your works
The dawn of radiant light.

By your command the day was named
From dawn to dusk its span.
As darkness falls we place our lives
Within your gracious hand.

Unto your courts may we approach,
The prize of life to win;
Avoiding every evil path,
O keep us free from sin.

O loving Father, hear our prayer,
Through Christ, your only Son,
Who with the Spirit ever lives,
Three persons, Godhead one. Amen.

> — Text: *Lucis Creator optime,* 7th–8th century; trans. Frank C.
> Quinn, O.P., alt. © 1989, GIA Publications, Inc.

Psalm 124   PRAISE OF GOD'S LIBERATING POWER

Antiphon: Blessed be the Lord, who made heaven and earth.

If it had not been the Lord who was on our side —
let Israel now say —
if it had not been the Lord who was on our side,
when foes rose up against us,
then they would have swallowed us up alive,
when their anger was kindled against us;
then the flood would have swept us away,
then the torrent would have gone over us;
then the raging waters would have gone over us.

Blessed be the Lord,
who has not given us
as prey to their teeth!
We have escaped as a bird
from the snare of the fowlers;
the snare is broken,
and we have escaped!
Our help is in the name of the Lord
who made heaven and earth.

Antiphon: Blessed be the Lord who made heaven and earth.

Prayer

> *Leader:* Let us pray (*pause for quiet prayer*)
>
> > God of might and majesty,
> > fill your church with life,
> > the church that puts its trust
> > in the power of your name.
> > Make it a champion of justice
> > and rescue it from its enemies;
> > in Jesus' name.
>
> *All:* ~*Amen.*

Reading PRAYER AND THANKSGIVING *Philippians 4:4–7*

Rejoice in the Lord always; again I say, Rejoice! Let your gentleness be known to everyone. The Lord is near. Do not worry about anything, but in everything by prayer and supplication with thanksgiving let your requests be made known to God. And the peace of God, which surpasses all understanding, will guard your hearts and minds in Christ Jesus.

Pause for meditation

Response

> *Leader:* Though I walk in darkness
>
> > *All:* ~*The Lord is my light.*

A Pauline Canticle   *1 Timothy 3:16; 6:15–16*

Antiphon: Great is the mystery of our religion!

Christ was revealed in flesh,
vindicated in spirit,
seen by angels,
proclaimed among Gentiles,
believed in throughout the world,
taken up in glory.

He is the blessed and only Sovereign,
the King of kings and the Lord of lords.
He alone has immortality
and dwells in unapproachable light,
whom no one has ever seen or can see;
to him be honor and eternal dominion. Amen.

Antiphon: Great is the mystery of our religion!

Litany

Leader: Like travelers lost in a parched and burning desert,

All: *~We cry unto you, O Lord.*

Like those shipwrecked on a lonely coast,
~We cry unto you, O Lord.

Like a mother robbed of a crust of bread
that she was bringing to her starving children,
~We cry unto you, O Lord.

Like a prisoner confined to a dank and gloomy dungeon,
~We cry unto you, O Lord.

Like a slave torn by his master's lash,
~We cry unto you, O Lord.

Like an innocent person led to execution.
~We cry unto you, O Lord.

Like all the nations of the earth
before their deliverance dawned,
~We cry unto you, O Lord.

Like Christ on the cross when he said:
"My God, my God, why have you forsaken me?"
~We cry unto you, O Lord.

Spontaneous prayers of intercession

Prayer

Leader: Lord Jesus, by your cross,
the church is redeemed and raised on high.
Protect us who take refuge
beneath the wings of your cross
and bathe us in the precious blood and water
that gushed from your pierced side,
O Savior of the world,
living and reigning for ever and ever.

All: *~Amen.*

Blessing

Leader: The grace of our Lord Jesus Christ,
and the love of God,
and the communion of the Holy Spirit,
+ be with us all.

All: *~Amen.*

⊗ FRIDAY MORNING PRAYER

In the Christian week, just as Sunday is devoted to the resurrection, Friday has been set apart to consider the passion and death of Jesus. These mysteries are not separate but intertwined; the cross is seen in the light of its fulfillment. Since Easter "the cross shines forth in mystic glow" and the body of the glorified Savior bears the still vivid marks of the five precious wounds.

Leader: We adore + your cross, O Lord,

All: *~And we praise and glorify your holy Resurrection.*

Leader: For by the wood of the cross,

All: *~Joy came into the whole world.*

Hymn

At this same hour, Redeemer King,
You climbed the cross, your royal throne;
Your arms embracing heaven and earth,
You claimed creation as your own.

This was your hour of trial, Lord,
When powers of darkness ruled the skies,
The darkest hour before the dawn
Of endless day in paradise.

Praise God the Father, fount of grace;
Praise God the Son, who set us free;
Praise God the Spirit, Lord of life;
Praise God, the Blessed Trinity. Amen.

> — Text: James Quinn, S.J., *Praise for All Seasons*
> (Kingston, N.Y.: Selah Publishing Co., 1994), p. 13

Canticle of Isaiah   *Isaiah 63:1–5*

Antiphon: The Son of God loved me
            and gave his life for me.

"Who is this that comes from Edom,
from Bozrah in garments stained crimson?
Who is this so splendidly robed,
marching in his great might?"

"It is I, announcing vindication,
mighty to save."

"Why are your robes red,
and your garments like theirs
who tread the wine press?"

"I have trodden the wine press alone,
and from the peoples no one was with me;
I trod them in my anger
and trampled them in my wrath;
their juice spattered on my garments,
and stained all my robes.

For the day of vengeance was in my heart,
and the year for my redeeming work had come.

I looked but there was no helper;
I stared, but there was no one to sustain me;
so my arm brought me victory,
and my wrath sustained me."

Antiphon: The Son of God loved me
and gave his life for me.

Prayer

Leader: Let us pray (*pause for quiet prayer*)

Lord Jesus Christ,
stretched out on the cross for us
and pierced with five grievous wounds,
be a mighty Savior for us
and bring us news of victory
in the hour of your triumph;
we ask this in your precious name.

All: ~*Amen.*

Reading   JESUS PROPHESIES HIS DEATH   *Mark 10:33–34*

Jesus said to the twelve: See, we are going up to Jerusalem, and
the Son of Man will be handed over to the chief priests and the
scribes, and they will condemn him to death; then they will hand
him over to the Gentiles; they will mock him, and spit upon him,
and flog him, and kill him; after three days he will rise again.

Pause for meditation

Response

Leader: In the cross is victory,

All: ~*In the cross is power.*

Canticle of St. Paul the Apostle   *Philippians 2:6–11*

Antiphon: Christ reigns from the noble tree of the cross!

Though he was in the form of God,
Jesus did not regard equality with God
as something to be exploited,
but emptied himself,

taking the form of a slave,
being born in human likeness.

And being found in human form,
Jesus humbled himself
and became obedient to the point of death —
even death on a cross.

Therefore God also highly exalted him
and gave him the name
that is above every name,

so that at the name of Jesus
every knee should bend,
in heaven and on earth
and under the earth,
and every tongue should confess
that Jesus Christ is Lord,
to the glory of God the Father.

Glory to the Father, and to the Son,
and to the Holy Spirit:

as it was in the beginning, is now,
and will be for ever. Amen.

Antiphon: Christ reigns from the noble tree of the cross!

Prayer

> *Leader:* Lord Jesus Christ,
> exposed to the gaze of all
> on the hill of Calvary,
> wash us in your precious blood
> and sign us with your mighty cross,
> raise up the dead who sleep in peace,
> and save us from the evil one,
> O Savior of the world,
> living and reigning for ever and ever.

> *All:* ~*Amen.*

Blessing

Leader: May the glorious passion of our Lord Jesus Christ
+ bring us to the joys of paradise.

All: ~Amen.

⍟ HOURS OF THE PASSION

In addition to morning and evening prayer, Friday has three brief memorials of the passion inspired by early Christian sources, especially by the Apostolic Tradition of St. Hippolytus of Rome, bishop and martyr, writing about 215 A.D.

MID-MORNING

Reading   Mark 15:22–26

The soldiers brought Jesus to the place called Golgotha (which means the place of the skull). And they offered him wine mixed with myrrh; but he did not take it. And they crucified him, and divided his clothes among them, casting lots to decide what each should take. It was nine o'clock in the morning when they crucified him. The inscription of the charge against him read, "The King of the Jews."

Leader: They have pierced my hands and my feet;

All: ~I can count all my bones.

Prayer

Leader: Lord Jesus Christ,
at mid-morning you were led to Golgotha
and nailed to the cross of pain
for the salvation of the world.
By the power of the cross,
forgive us our sins
and uproot all our sinful inclinations
that we may praise, love, and serve you,
now and for ever.

All: ~Amen.

NOON

Reading   Mark 15:26–33

With Jesus they crucified two bandits, one on his right and one on his left. Those who passed by derided him. . . . "He saved others; he cannot save himself. Let the Messiah, the King of Israel, come down from the cross now, so that we may see and believe." Those who were crucified with him also taunted him. When it was noon, darkness came over the whole land until three in the afternoon.

Leader: Standing near the cross of Jesus were his mother,

All: ~*And his mother's sister, and Mary Magdalene.*

Prayer

Leader: Lord Jesus Christ,
            as you hung on the cross at noon,
            daylight failed at the sight
            and darkness fell over the whole land.
            By the power of the cross,
            grant us lasting light for our souls and bodies
            and bring us in safety
            to the unfading glories of our heavenly home,
            where you live and reign for ever and ever.

All: ~*Amen.*

MID-AFTERNOON

Reading   Mark 15:33–34, 37–39

At three o'clock Jesus cried out with a loud voice, "My God, my God, why have you forsaken me? . . ." Then Jesus gave a loud cry and breathed his last. And the curtain of the temple was torn in two, from top to bottom. Now when the centurion, who stood facing him, saw that in this way he breathed his last, he said, "Truly this man was God's Son!"

Leader: Arise, O Christ, and help us,

All: ~*And deliver us for your name's sake.*

Prayer

Leader: Lord Jesus Christ,
as you were dying in agony at mid-afternoon,
you promised paradise to a repentant criminal,
handed over your spirit to your Father,
and descended among the dead for their enlightenment.
By the blood and water
that flowed from your pierced side,
wash away all our sins,
renew in us a new and life-giving spirit,
and bring us at last to the resurrection of the body
and life eternal in the world to come,
where you live and reign
with the Father and the Holy Spirit,
one God, for ever and ever.

All: *~Amen.*

◌ FRIDAY EVENING PRAYER

Leader: We adore + you, O Christ, and we bless you,

All: *~For by your holy cross, you have redeemed the world.*

Hymn

O sacred heart for all once broken,
Your precious blood for sinners shed,
Those words of love by you were spoken
That raised to life the living dead!

O heart, your love for all outpouring
In pain upon the cross you bled;
Come now with life, our life restoring,
O heart by which our hearts are fed!

— Text: James Quinn, S.J., *Praise for All Seasons*
(Kingston, N.Y.: Selah Publishing Co., 1994), p. 66

Psalm 142   GOD RESCUES HIS CHRIST

Antiphon: Christ is victor; Christ is ruler;
                   Christ is Lord of all!

With my voice I cry to the Lord,
I make supplication;
Before the Lord I tell my trouble,
I pour out my complaint.
When my spirit is faint,
you know my way.

In the path where I walk
they have hidden a trap for me.
Look on my right hand and see;
there is no one who takes notice of me;
no one cares for me.

I cry to you, O Lord;
I say, "You are my refuge,
my portion in the land of the living."
Give heed to my cry;
for I am brought very low.
Save me from my persecutors;
for they are too strong for me.

Bring me out of prison,
so that I may give thanks to your name!
The righteous will surround me,
for you will deal richly with me.

Antiphon: Christ is victor, Christ is ruler,
                   Christ is Lord of all!

Prayer

   Leader: Let us pray (*pause for quiet prayer*)

                 Lord Jesus Christ,
                 you loved us and offered yourself up for us,
                 as an agreeable and fragrant sacrifice to God.
                 Deliver us from our former darkness
                 and teach us to conduct ourselves
                 as children of the light

in all goodness, justice, and truth;
you live and reign for ever and ever.

All: ~Amen.

Reading   THE GOSPEL IN MINIATURE   *John 3:14–17*

Just as Moses lifted up the serpent in the wilderness, so must the
Son of Man be lifted up, that whoever believes in him may have
eternal life. For God so loved the world that he gave his only Son,
so that everyone who believes in him may not perish but may have
eternal life. God did not send his Son into the world to condemn
the world, but in order that the world might be saved through him.

Pause for meditation

Response

Leader: Let us glory in the cross of our Lord Jesus Christ,

All: ~For in him is our salvation, life, and resurrection.

Canticle of St. Peter the Apostle   *1 Peter 2:21–25*

Antiphon: With Christ I am nailed to the cross.

Christ suffered for you,
leaving you an example,
so that you should follow
in his steps.

He committed no sin,
and no deceit
was found in his mouth.

When he was abused,
he did not return abuse;
when he suffered,
he did not threaten;
but he entrusted himself
to the One who judges justly.

He himself bore our sins
in his body on the cross,
so that, free from sins,
we might live for righteousness;

by his wounds
you have been healed.

For you were going astray like sheep,
but now you have returned
to the shepherd and guardian of your souls.

Glory to God, Source of all being,
eternal Word, and Holy Spirit:

as it was in the beginning, is now,
and will be for ever. Amen.

Antiphon: With Christ I am nailed to the cross.

Litany

      Leader: Lord Jesus, Savior of the world,
               stir up your strength and help us,

         All: ~*We humbly pray.*

             By your cross and precious blood
             you have set us free; save us and help us,
             ~*We humbly pray.*

             You saved your disciples
             when they were ready to perish;
             hear us and save us,
             ~*We humbly pray.*

             In great mercy set us free from our sins,
             ~*We humbly pray.*

             Make it apparent that you are our Savior
             and mighty Deliverer that we may praise you,
             ~*We humbly pray.*

             Draw near according to your promise
             from your throne of glory,
             ~*We humbly pray.*

             Come again and live among us
             and stay with us for ever,
             ~*We humbly pray.*

And when you appear among us
with power and great glory
make us members of your victorious kingdom,
~*We humbly pray.*

— *Salvator Mundi,* trans. William G. Storey

Spontaneous prayers of intercession

Prayer

Leader: Lord Jesus Christ, Son of the living God,
set your passion, your cross, and your death
between your judgment and our souls,
now and at the hour of our death.
In your goodness,
grant mercy and grace to the living
and forgiveness and rest to the dead;
to the church and to the nations peace and concord
and to us sinners life and glory without end.

All: ~*Amen.*

Blessing

Leader: May the glorious passion of our Lord Jesus Christ
+ bring us to the joys of paradise.

All: ~*Amen.*

❦ SATURDAY MORNING PRAYER

This is the last day of the Christian week, which is often dedicated to the mystery of the incarnation in that the eternal Word
of God took flesh in the womb of the Virgin Mary. Now and for
ever he is the God-Man who bridges the gap between the eternal
and the temporal, the infinite and the finite, the lasting and the
passing. Jesus is the supreme bridge builder by whom we can cross
from this world of shadows to the land of everlasting peace and
happiness.

When Mary consented in faith to the message of the angel
Gabriel and became the mother of the incarnate Savior, she began
her intimate collaboration with her Son in all the saving acts of his
life. As the new Eve, she cooperated with the new Adam to bring

about the renewal of the world. In union with the other devout women who had accompanied Jesus from Galilee to Jerusalem, she stood beneath the cross as he suffered and died, was bestowed on the beloved disciple, and awaited in prayer for the coming of the Holy Spirit on Pentecost. Our weekly memorial of the incarnation is a thanksgiving to her Son for the cross, the resurrection, and the Pentecost that continues in all our lives.

Leader: O Lord, + open my lips.

All: ~*And my mouth will proclaim your praise.*

Hymn

The God whom earth and sea and sky
Adore and praise and magnify,
Whose might they claim, whose love they tell,
In Mary's body comes to dwell.

O Mother blest! the chosen shrine
Wherein the Architect divine,
Whose hand contains the earth and sky,
Has come in human form to lie.

Blest in the message Gabriel brought;
Blest in the work the Spirit wrought;
Most blest, to bring to human birth
The long desired of all the earth.

O Lord, the Virgin-born, to you
Eternal praise and laud are due,
Whom with the Father we adore
And Spirit blest for evermore. Amen.

> — Text: *Quem terra, pontus, aethera,* Venantius Fortunatus
> (530–609); trans. John Mason Neale (1818–1866), alt.

Canticle of Judith   *Judith 13:18–20; 15:9*

Antiphon: All generations will call me blessed.

The Most High God has blessed you
more than any woman in the world.
How worthy of praise is the Lord God
who created heaven and earth.

He guided you as you cut off the head
of our deadliest enemy.

Your trust in God will never be forgotten
by those who tell of God's power.
May God give you everlasting honor
for what you have done.

May he reward you with blessings
because you remained faithful to him.
And did not hesitate to risk your own life
to relieve the oppression of your people.

You are Jerusalem's crowning glory,
the heroine of Israel,
the pride and joy of our people.

Antiphon: All generations will call me blessed.

Prayer

Leader: Let us pray (*pause for quiet prayer*)

Loving Savior,
by the cooperation and heroic faith of Mary,
the valiant woman of the Gospel,
you crushed the head of our ancient enemy
and set all things under your feet.
By her undying fidelity,
make her the pride and joy of Christians
and the crowning glory of your people.
You live and reign for ever and ever.

All: ~*Amen.*

Reading GOD WITH US *Isaiah 7:14; 9:6, 7*

The Lord himself will give you a sign. Look, the young woman is
with child, and shall bear a son, and shall name him Immanuel
(God with us).... For a child has been born for us, a son given to
us; and he is named Wonderful Counselor, Mighty God, Everlasting
Father, Prince of Peace. The zeal of the Lord of hosts will do this.

Pause for meditation

Response

> *Leader:* Blest is the womb that bore you, O Christ, alleluia!
>
> *All:* ~*And blest the breasts that nursed you, alleluia!*

Canticle of Zachary   *Luke 1:68–79*

Antiphon: Blest is the Virgin Mary who believed
             that nothing is impossible with God.

Blest be + the God of Israel
who comes to set us free
and raises up new hope for us:
a Branch for David's tree.

So have the prophets long declared
that with a mighty arm
God would turn back our enemies
and all who wish us harm.

With promised mercy will God still
the covenant recall,
the oath once sworn to Abraham
from foes to save us all;

that we might worship without fear
and offer fervent praise,
in holiness and righteousness
to serve God all our days.

My child, as prophet of the Lord,
you will prepare the way,
to tell God's people they are saved
from sin's eternal sway.

Then shall God's mercy from on high
shine forth and never cease
to drive away the gloom of death
and lead us into peace.

Antiphon: Blest is the Virgin Mary who believed
             that nothing is impossible with God.

— Words: Carl P. Daw, Jr.
Words © 1989 by Hope Publishing Co.

Prayer

Leader: Only begotten Son and eternal Word of God,
you took flesh of the Blessed Virgin Mary
and became man for our sake.
You willingly endured the cross for us,
overcame death by your own death,
rose again on the third day,
and opened for us the way to eternal life,
where you live and reign in glory
with the Father and the Holy Spirit,
one God, now and for ever.

All: ~*Amen.*

Blessing

Leader: May the Word made flesh, full of grace and truth,
+ bless us and keep us.

All: ~*Amen.*

◎ SATURDAY EVENING PRAYER

Leader: Come, let us adore the Word made flesh,

All: ~*Christ Jesus, the Son of the Virgin Mary.*

Hymn

Sing of Mary, pure and lowly,
Virgin Mother undefiled.
Sing of God's own Son most holy,
Who became her little child.

Fairest child of fairest mother,
God the Lord who came to earth
Word made flesh, our very brother,
Takes our nature by his birth.

Sing of Jesus, son of Mary,
In the home at Nazareth.
Toil and labor cannot weary
Love enduring unto death.

Constant was the love he gave her,
Though he went forth from her side,
Forth to preach and heal and suffer,
Till on Calvary he died.

Glory be to God the Father,
Glory be to God the Son;
Glory be to God the Spirit;
Glory to the Three in One.

> — Roland F. Palmer, S.S.J.E. (1891–1985),
> © Estate of R. F. Palmer

Canticle of Isaiah   *Isaiah 66:10–14*

Antiphon: I will comfort you, says the Lord,
          as a mother comforts her child.

Rejoice with Jerusalem; be glad for her,
all you that love this city!
Rejoice with her now,
all you that have mourned for her!

You will enjoy her prosperity,
like a child at its mother's breast.

The Lord says,
"I will bring you lasting prosperity;
the wealth of the nations
will flow to you like a river
that never goes dry.

You will be like a child
that is nursed by its mother,
carried in her arms,
and treated with love.

I will comfort you in Jerusalem,
as a mother comforts her child.
When you see this happen,
you will be glad;
it will make you strong and healthy."

Antiphon: I will comfort you, says the Lord,
          as a mother nurses her child.

Prayer

Leader: Let us pray (*pause for quiet prayer*)

Lord Jesus,
in your dying moments
you bequeathed your holy Mother
to your beloved disciple
and to the church at large.
As we recall her broken heart,
may we share her great faith and joy
in your rising again on the third day.
You are the Lord of the living and of the dead,
now and for ever.

All: ~*Amen.*

Reading MARY AT THE FOOT OF THE CROSS *John 19:25–27*

Standing near the cross of Jesus were his mother, and his mother's sister, Mary the wife of Clopas, and Mary Magdalene. When Jesus saw his mother and the disciple whom he loved standing beside her, he said to his mother, "Woman, here is your son." Then he said to the disciple, "Here is your mother." And from that hour the disciple took her into his own home.

Pause for meditation

Response

Leader: Blessed are you among women, O Mary,

All: ~*And blessed is the fruit of your womb, Jesus.*

Canticle of the Blessed Virgin Mary *Luke 1:46–55*

Antiphon: A great sign appeared in the heavens:
a woman clothed with the sun,
with the moon under her feet,
and on her head a crown of twelve stars,
alleluia! (Revelation 12:1)

My soul + proclaims the greatness of the Lord,
my spirit rejoices in God my Savior,
for you, Lord, have looked with favor
on your lowly servant.

From this day all generations will call me blessed:
you, the Almighty, have done great things for me
and holy is your name.
You have mercy on those who fear you,
from generation to generation.

You have shown strength with your arm
and scattered the proud in their conceit,
casting down the mighty from their thrones
and lifting up the lowly.
You have filled the hungry with good things
and sent the rich away empty.

You have come to the aid of your servant Israel,
to remember the promise of mercy,
the promise made to our forebears,
to Abraham and his children for ever.

Glory to the Father, and to the Son,
and to the Holy Spirit:

as it was in the beginning, is now,
and will be for ever. Amen.

Antiphon: A great sign appeared in the heavens:
a woman clothed with the sun,
with the moon under her feet,
and on her head a crown of twelve stars,
alleluia!

Litany

Leader: Lord Jesus Christ, Son of God and Son of Mary,

All: ~*Hear us and have mercy.*

Lord Jesus Christ, who sent an angel to Mary
to announce your incarnation,
~*Hear us and have mercy.*

Lord Jesus Christ, who lived in subjection
to Mary and Joseph at Nazareth,
~*Hear us and have mercy.*

Lord Jesus Christ, whose Mother stood fast
at the foot of the cross,
~Hear us and have mercy.

Lord Jesus Christ, who brought your Mother into glory,
~Hear us and have mercy.

Lord Jesus Christ, who willed that your Mother
be revered in every generation,
~Hear us and have mercy.

Spontaneous prayers of intercession

Prayer

Leader: Gracious God and Father,
you have taken to yourself the blessed Virgin Mary,
Mother of your incarnate Son:
Grant that we, who have been redeemed by his blood,
may share with her the glory of your eternal kingdom;
through Jesus Christ our Lord,
who lives and reigns with you and the Holy Spirit,
one God, now and for ever.

All: *~Amen.*

— *Book of Common Prayer* (1979), p. 243

Blessing

Leader: May Christ, our incarnate Savior,
+ bring us into his endless kingdom.

All: *~Amen.*

Three

PRAYERS FOR ALL AGES AND SEASONS

⚮ SELF-SURRENDER

Father,
I surrender myself into your hands;
do with me what you will.
Whatever you do, I thank you:
I am ready for all, I accept all.
Let only your will be done in me,
and in all your creatures —
I wish no more than this, O Lord.
Into your hands I commend my spirit;
I offer it to you with all the love of my heart,
for I love you, Lord,
and so need to give myself,
to surrender myself into your hands without reserve,
and with boundless confidence,
for you are my Father.

— Charles de Foucauld (1858–1916)

⚮ SELF-OFFERING

Lord, I freely yield all my liberty to you.
Take my memory, my intellect, and my entire will.
You have given me everything I am or have;
I give it all back to you to stand under your will alone.
Your love and your grace are enough for me;
I shall ask for nothing more.

— St. Ignatius Loyola (1491–1556)

✑ TRANSFORMATION

O my divine Savior,
transform me into yourself.
May my hands be the hands of Jesus,
may my tongue be the tongue of Jesus.
Grant that every faculty of my body
may serve only to glorify you.
Above all, transform my soul and all its powers
that my memory, my will, and my affections
may be the memory, the will, and the affections of Jesus.
Destroy in me all that is not of you.
Grant that I may live only in you and by you and for you
that I may truly say with Saint Paul:
"I live now, not I, but Christ lives in me."

— Blessed John Gabriel Perboyre, C.M. (1802–1840)

✑ TRUST AND CONFIDENCE

My Lord God,
I have no idea where I am going.
I do not see the road ahead of me.
I cannot know for certain where it will end.
Nor do I really know myself,
and the fact that I think that I am following your will
does not mean that I am actually doing so.
But I believe that the desire to please you does in fact please you.
And I hope that I have that desire in all that I am doing.
I hope that I will never do anything apart from that desire.
And I know that if I do this,
you will lead me by the right road
though I may know nothing about it.
Therefore I will trust you always
though I may seem to be lost
and in the shadow of death.
I will not fear, for you are ever with me,
and you will never leave me
to face my perils alone.

— Thomas Merton (1915–1968)

◈ TO CHRIST OUR ONLY TEACHER

Thank you, Jesus, for bringing me this far.
In your light I see the light of my life.
Your teaching is brief and to the point:
You persuade us to trust in our heavenly Father;
you command us to love one another.
What is easier than to believe in God?
What is sweeter than to love him?
Your yoke is pleasant, your burden is light,
you, the one and only teacher!
You promise everything to those who obey your teaching;
you ask nothing too hard for a believer,
nothing a lover can refuse.
Your promises to your disciples are true,
entirely true, nothing but the truth.
Even more, you promise us yourself,
the perfection of all that can be made perfect.
Thank you, Jesus, now and always. Amen.

— Nicholas of Cusa (1401–1464)

◈ TO CHRIST OUR KING

Lord Jesus Christ,
you are the king of the whole world.
All that was made was created for you.
Exercise your sovereign rights over me.
I renew my baptismal vows,
renouncing Satan with all his works and false glamour,
and I promise to live as a good Christian.
In particular, I pledge myself to do all in my power
to make the rights of God and of your church
triumph in the world.
Divine Heart of Jesus,
I offer you whatever I can do
to get all human hearts to admit your sacred lordship
so that the kingdom of your peace will be established
throughout the whole world. Amen.

— Pope Pius XI (1922–1939)

❧ FOR COURAGE

Lord Jesus, teach me to be generous;
teach me to serve you as you deserve,
to give and not to count the cost,
to fight and not to heed the wounds,
to work and not to seek for rest,
to labor and not to seek reward,
except that of knowing that I do your will. Amen.

— St. Ignatius of Loyola (1491–1556)

❧ GRACE TO KNOW YOU

Gracious and holy Father,
please give me:
intellect to understand you,
reason to discern you,
diligence to seek you,
wisdom to find you,
a spirit to know you,
a heart to meditate upon you,
ears to hear you, eyes to see you,
a tongue to proclaim you,
a way of life pleasing to you,
patience to wait for you
and perseverance to look for you.
Grant me a perfect end —
your holy presence,
a blessed resurrection,
and life everlasting.

— Attributed to St. Benedict of Nursia (ca. 480–555)

❧ FOR GUIDANCE

God of our life,
there are days when the burdens we carry
chafe our shoulders and weigh us down;
when the road seems dreary and endless,
the skies gray and threatening;

when our lives have no music in them,
and our hearts are lonely,
and our souls have lost their courage.
Flood our path with light,
turn our eyes to where the skies are full of promise;
tune our hearts to brave music;
give us a sense of comradeship
with the saints and heroes of every age;
quicken our spirits
that we may be able to encourage
the souls of all who journey with us
on the road of life,
to your honor and glory.

— Attributed to St. Augustine of Hippo (354–430)

ℛ FOR GOOD CHOICES

Abba, dear Father,
you are the creative origin of all that I am
and of all I am called to be.
With the talents and opportunities I have,
how may I serve you best?
Please guide my mind and heart,
open me to the needs of my country
and of the world,
and help me to choose wisely and practically
for your honor and glory,
and for the good of all those whose lives I touch.

ℛ PRAYER FOR PEACE

Lord, make me a instrument of your peace:
where there is hatred, let me sow love;
where there is injury, pardon;
where there is doubt, faith;
where there is despair, hope;
where there is darkness, light;
and where there is sadness, joy.

O divine Master, grant that I may not so much seek
to be consoled as to console,
to be understood as to understand,
to be loved as to love.

For it is in giving that we receive,
it is in pardoning that we are pardoned,
and it is in dying that we are born to eternal life.

— Attributed to St. Francis of Assisi (1181–1226)

❧ FOR THE CHRISTIAN CHURCH

Gracious Father,
we pray to you for your holy catholic church.
Fill it with your truth.
Keep it in your peace.
Where it is corrupt, reform it.
Where it is in error, correct it.
Where it is right, defend it.
Where it is in want, provide for it.
Where it is divided, reunite it;
for the sake of your Son,
our Savior Jesus Christ. Amen.

— William Laud, archbishop of Canterbury (1573–1645)

❧ FOR MY FAMILY

Lord Jesus Christ,
I praise and thank you for my parents
and for my brothers and sisters
whom you have given me to cherish.
Surround them with your tender, loving care,
teach them to love and serve one another
and to look to you in all their needs.
I place them all in your care,
knowing that your love for them is greater than my own.
Keep us close to one another in this life
and conduct us at last to our true and heavenly home,
where you live and reign with the Father and the Holy Spirit,
one God, for ever and ever. Amen.

❧ FOR FRIENDS IN TROUBLE

God of love,
you care for us in all circumstances.
Be a friend to all my friends,
and especially to those in trouble.
The stresses and strains of life
are sometimes too much for them,
and they need to experience your loving care.
Give the friendless at least one timely friend.
Give the jobless a new opportunity for useful work.
Give the sick healing and fresh strength.
Give the dying hope and consolation,
now and at the hour of their death.
Good Lord,
help them all in their time of need
and make us friends together
in time and in eternity;
in the name of Jesus. Amen.

❧ FOR GOOD SEXUAL ATTITUDES

In the Apostles' Creed
we say that you are the Creator of heaven and earth
and that your Son assumed our full human nature.
Since he was made flesh for our sake,
you must know more about sex than we do!
Sex must be a part of your lovely plan for us.
Your Son was a sexual being like us,
and the truth about human sexuality
must come from a deeper and fuller understanding
of the Word-made-flesh
who came and lived among us.

Help me to appreciate and embrace my sexual orientation
without fear or shame.
Because my sexuality is your personal gift to me,
help me to accept it graciously, and to use it wisely and well,
with full human responsibility.
And that is asking a lot! Amen.

ॐ **FOR A PARTICULAR FRIENDSHIP**

Lord God,
when you created me in my mother's womb,
you fashioned me as a sexual being
with all the longings and desires
that are part of such a state.

As I grow into the fuller possession of my humanity,
of my powers of understanding and affection,
I want to offer them back to you
as an appropriate sacrifice of praise and thanksgiving.
You have created me to share my life with one particular person.
Although there are many whom I could love
there is one alone to whom I shall pledge my life.
I am confident that I shall meet such a person in good time.

Ready me for such an encounter,
prepare me with gifts of mind and body,
fill me with expectation and discernment,
and help me to rely upon you alone
with humility and earnest desire!

ॐ **FOR A PARTNER**

Heavenly Father,
from the very beginning
you created human beings to discover love
and to express it in creative unions
of affection and mutual service.
Your mystery of love is reflected
in our faithful love for one another.
Help us to prepare seriously for such a blessing.
Give us sensitive hearts, discerning minds, and ready wills,
eager to serve you and to discover the truth of one another.
Nourish our burgeoning sexuality
and direct it to good and honorable ends
worthy to be offered to you honestly and without shame.
Unite us before your altar, feed us with your body and blood,
and become the common center of our hearts and homes. Amen.

◌ **FOR THE FORGIVENESS OF SINS**

Lord Jesus Christ, whose will all things obey:
Pardon what I have done wrong
and grant that I may sin no more.
Lord, I believe that though I do not deserve it,
you can cleanse me of all my sins.
Lord, I know that people look at the face
but that you see the heart.
Send your Spirit into my innermost being,
to take possession of my soul and body.
Without you I cannot be saved.
With you to protect me
I long for your saving help.
And now I ask for wisdom.
Of your great goodness help and defend me.
Guide my heart, Almighty God,
that I may remember your Presence
both by day and by night. Amen.

— An Ancient Prayer

◌ **INVOCATION OF THE HOLY SPIRIT**

Leader: Come, Holy Spirit, fill the hearts of your faithful

All: ~*And kindle in them the fire of your divine love.*

When you send forth your Spirit, they are created,
~*And you renew the face of the earth.*

Let us pray (*pause for quiet reflection*)

God of fire and light,
on the first Pentecost
you taught the hearts of your disciples
by the light of the Holy Spirit.
Under the inspiration of that same Spirit,
give us a taste for what is right and true,
and a continuing experience
of his joy-bringing presence and power;
through Jesus Christ our Lord.
~*Amen.*

FOR HEALING

Lord Jesus,
healer of our souls and bodies,
during your life on earth,
you went about doing good,
healing every manner of sickness and disease,
strengthening, curing, comforting, and consoling.
You want to see us healthy and happy;
you are the enemy of sickness and disease,
and in and through you they are overcome and conquered.
Lay your healing hands upon us now,
so that we may live in your praise untiringly. Amen.

IN TIME OF SICKNESS

Lord Jesus, you suffered and died for me;
you understand suffering and you share it with us.
Teach me to accept my pains,
to bear them in union with you,
and to offer them up for the forgiveness of my sins
and for the welfare of the living and the dead.
Calm my fears, increase my trust in you;
make me patient and cooperative with those who serve me,
and if it be your will,
restore me to health,
so that I may live and work for your honor and glory
and for the good of all. Amen.

YOUR WILL BE DONE

God and loving Creator,
your will be done,
on earth as it is in heaven.
I offer my sickness with all its sufferings to you,
together with all that my Savior has suffered for me.

By the power of his pain-filled passion,
have mercy on me
and free me from this illness and pain,

if it be according to your holy will
and for my ultimate good.
Lord, I entrust my life and my death to you;
in sickness and in health,
I want only to love you always. Amen.

◈ FOR THE GIFT OF FINAL PERSEVERANCE

Noble Jesus,
you have graciously granted me
the gift of your holy teaching.
Of your great goodness
help me to come at length to you,
the fount of all wisdom,
and to live in your presence
for ever. Amen.

— St. Bede the Venerable (673–735)

◈ PRAYER FOR A PEACEFUL DEATH

Lord Jesus Christ,
you desire everyone's salvation
and no one ever appeals to you in vain,
for with your own lips you promised:
"Whatever you ask the Father in my name, I will do."
In your name — Jesus, Savior —
I ask that in my dying moments
you will give me full use of my senses,
heart-felt sorrow for my sins,
firm faith, hope in good measure, and perfect love,
that I may be able to say honestly to you:
"Into your hands, O Lord, I commend my spirit.
You have redeemed me, Lord God of truth."

— St. Vincent Ferrer (1350–1419)

∂ **FOR THOSE WHO HAVE GONE BEFORE US**

Leader: The Lord will open to them the gates of paradise,

All: *and they will return to that homeland*
where there is no death but only lasting joy.

Eternal rest grant to them, O Lord,
~*And let perpetual light shine upon them.*

Let us pray (*pause for quiet prayer*)

O God, our Creator and Redeemer,
you raised Christ from the dead
and brought him into glory.
May all who have gone before us,
believing in him and his power to save,
share in his victory over death
and come to enjoy the light of glory
in union with all his saints;
through the same Christ our Lord.
~*Amen.*

May the souls of the faithful departed
through the mercy of God rest in peace.
~*Amen.*

∂ **FOR THE FAITHFUL DEPARTED**

By the merits of your rising from the dead,
Lord Christ,
let death no longer have dominion
over those who have gone before us in faith.
Grant to your servants a resting place
in your everlasting mansions
and in the arms of Abraham,
our father in the faith.

Grant this to all who have served you
in purity of heart and with a clear conscience —
to our mothers and fathers,
to our sisters and brothers,
to our friends and relatives.

Prepare a place in your heavenly kingdom
for everyone who has served you faithfully
in this present life,
and to all who, in their own way,
have tried to do your will. Amen.

— An Ancient Prayer

☙ **FOR THOSE WHO MOURN**

Lord Jesus,
you wept at the grave of Lazarus
and told his sisters:
"I am the resurrection and the life."
Your sympathy and your assurance
are what we need in the face of death.
Visit our mourning hearts and homes,
console us with the sight of your tears,
and make us cling to your promises
as we put our faith in your glorious resurrection.
Blessed be the name of Jesus! Amen.

☙ **PSALM 130 — DE PROFUNDIS**

Out of the depths I cry to you, O Lord!
Lord, hear my voice!
Let your ears be attentive
to the voice of my supplications!

If you, O Lord, should mark iniquities,
Lord, who could stand?
But there is forgiveness with you,
that you may be worshiped.

I wait for the Lord, my soul waits,
in the Lord's word I hope;
my soul waits for the Lord
more than watchers for the morning,
more than watchers for the morning.

O Israel, hope in the Lord!
For with the Lord there is steadfast love;

with the Lord there is great redemption.
The Lord alone will redeem Israel
from all iniquities.

Leader: Eternal rest grant to them, O Lord,

All: *~And let perpetual light shine upon them.*

Let us pray for all our departed friends and relatives:

Abba, God of loving kindness,
through the merits of Christ Jesus, our Savior,
deliver from everlasting death
all our friends, relatives, and benefactors, *N*_____.
Guide them into the land of perpetual peace
where you live and reign in everlasting splendor,
now and always and for ever and ever.
~Amen.

∞ FOR THOSE WE LOVE

Lord God,
we can hope for others nothing better
than the happiness we want for ourselves.
Therefore, I pray you,
do not separate me after death,
from those whom I have loved on earth.
Grant that where I am they may also be,
and let me enjoy their presence in heaven
after being so often deprived of it on earth.

Lord God,
I ask you to receive your dear children
immediately into your sacred heart.
After this brief life on earth,
give them eternal happiness.

— St. Ambrose of Milan (334–397)

◌ **DOXOLOGY**

To God the Father,
who loved us and made us accepted in the Beloved:

To God the Son,
who loved us and loosed us from our sins by his own blood:

To God the Holy Spirit,
who sheds the love of God abroad in our hearts:

To the One True God,
be all love and all glory for time and for eternity. Amen.

— Bishop Thomas Ken (1631–1711)

Four

DEVOTIONS FOR SPECIAL MOMENTS AND SPECIAL DAYS

Gay and lesbian homes and families come in a variety of forms: a single parent with one or more children, a couple with or without children, gay or lesbian grandparents with children. In addition, many gay and lesbian people are single and without children but establish admirable and hospitable homes frequented by loving friends and relatives. Whatever form it takes, the Christian home is the primary unit of church life. St. Augustine of Hippo called it an *ecclesiola,* a church in miniature.

When we celebrate the meaningful occasions of our common existence, whether in church or in the home, these special moments become highlights of our Christian experience. Since so many gay and lesbian people suffer rejection and expulsion from their families of birth, it is important to seize these occasions and honor their significance.

☙ SOME SUGGESTIONS

The following scripturally inspired rituals are simple, dynamic aids to personal or group prayer.

The highlighted rubrics and other directions for group use are included to facilitate participation by several people praying together. It is suggested that:

- the recitation of hymns, psalms, and canticles be alternated between the leader of prayer and the whole group;

- the antiphon before a psalm or canticle be recited by all in unison;
- the antiphon be repeated in full by everyone after the psalm or canticle;
- the sign of the cross be made where a "+" occurs in the text;
- lines introduced by a tilde (~) be recited by all.

A Christian never really prays alone. As baptized members of the church, we pray in union with the whole church, the communion of saints. Individuals, of course, enjoy greater freedom of posture and ceremony but should be mindful of the reverence that is brought to the prayer.

Communal prayer requires sensitivity to the needs of the group. It is always quality and not quantity that matters in prayer. This is particularly true when children are present or when we gather in prayer to support a sick or dying friend. Selecting a few elements from a service can often be more prayerful than attempting to complete the whole service.

Likewise, standing, sitting, and kneeling may be arranged according to the nature of the group. For more formal gatherings, the following is suggested: *stand* until the readings, *sit* for the readings, *stand* again for the canticle, and *kneel* for the intercessions and blessing.

❧ A COMING-OUT PARTY

A crucial event in the life of a gay or lesbian person is the personal, interior recognition of that person's sexual orientation. Sometimes, many years pass before this can become clear. Coming-out to oneself gradually leads to a second crucial event: coming-out to others. At first this is usually done one person at a time: to a close friend, to a brother or sister, to one's father or mother, to one's co-workers, etc. The third event can be a party for all those who have supported a person in his or her decision to come out. This event is a communal celebration of the recognition we all need and deserve.

Like baptism, it is a kind of rebirth for the individual person and for the community of friends who surround and support the individual who has chosen to come out. It can, of course, be a small, intimate gathering of friends and relatives or it can be a much larger and public event. Often, too, it will include two people; the person coming out may no longer be alone and may have a partner/lover/spouse/life-companion. In any case the celebration deserves a Christian setting.

The Leader of the celebration might well be a lesbian or gay mentor who was crucial to the decision process or some other close friend who is comfortable in a public role. Three different people might serve as readers of the three Scripture lessons. The Leader and the person who is coming out may choose to stand facing their friends across a table holding a cross, candles, flowers, and a Bible.

Leader: Together with our friend, *N*_____, let us celebrate this coming-out party in the name of God: Creator, + Redeemer, and abiding Spirit.

All: ~*Amen.*

Leader: Let us recite Psalm 34 in alternate stanzas.

Psalm 34:1–14   PRAISE GOD'S GOODNESS

I will bless the Lord at all times;
God's praise shall continually be in my mouth.
My life makes its boast in the Lord;
let the afflicted hear and be glad.

O magnify the Lord with me,
and let us exalt God's name together!
I sought the Lord, who answered me,
and delivered me from all my fears.

Look to God and be radiant,
so your faces shall never be ashamed.
The poor cried out, and the Lord heard,
and saved them out of all their troubles.

The angel of the Lord encamps
around those who fear God, and delivers them.
O taste and see that the Lord is good!
Happy are those who take refuge in God!

O fear the Lord, you holy ones,
for those who fear God have no want.

The young lions suffer want and hunger,
but those who seek the Lord lack no good thing.

Come, O children, listen to me,
I will teach you the fear of the Lord.
Which of you desires life
and covets many days to enjoy good?

Keep your tongue from evil,
and your lips from speaking deceit.
Depart from evil, and do good;
seek peace, and pursue it.

Prayer

> *Leader:* Let us pray (*pause for quiet prayer*)

> God of our ancestors in the faith,
> you love honesty and courage
> and support those who speak the truth.
> Help us to rejoice in the coming out
> of our dear friend, *N*_____,
> and to thank him/her for the honesty and integrity
> that encourage and support us all.
> Send your Holy Spirit
> to hover over our hearts and our homes
> to put a new and noble spirit
> in our lives and our affections
> that we may love and serve you
> and those who surround us,
> today and every day of the years to come.
> We ask this through Jesus Christ, our Lord.

> *All:* ~Amen.

Each Scripture reading may be taken by a different reader.

First Reading   GOD'S CHILDREN   *Galatians 3:23–29*

Before the time for faith came, the Law kept us all locked up as
prisoners until this coming faith should be revealed. And so the
Law was in charge of us until Christ came, in order that we might
then be put right with God through faith. Now that the time for
faith is here, the Law is no longer in charge of us. It is through

faith that all of you are God's children in union with Christ Jesus. You were baptized in union with Christ, and now you are clothed, so to speak, with the life of Christ himself. So there is no difference between Jews and Gentiles, between slaves and free people, between men and women [between black and white, between gay and straight]; you are all one in union with Christ Jesus. If you belong to Christ, then you are the descendants of Abraham and will receive what God has promised.
This is the Word of the Lord.

> *All: ~Thanks be to God*

Second Reading LOVE ONE ANOTHER *Romans 13:8–10*

Be under obligation to no one — the only obligation you have is to love one another. Whoever does this has obeyed the Law. The commandments, "Do not commit adultery; do not commit murder; do not steal; do not desire what belongs to someone else" — all these, and any other besides, are summed up in the one command, "Love your neighbor as you love yourself." If you love others, you will never do them wrong; to love, then, is to obey the whole Law.
This is the Word of the Lord.

> *All: ~Thanks be to God*

Gospel Reading THE BEATITUDES *Luke 6:20–23*

Jesus looked at his disciples and said,
Happy are you poor;
the Kingdom of God is yours!
Happy are you who are hungry now;
you will be filled!
Happy are you who weep now;
you will laugh!
Happy are you when people hate you, reject you,
insult you, and say that you are evil,
all because of the Son of Man!
Be glad when that happens and dance for joy,
because a great reward is kept for you in heaven.
For their ancestors did the very same things
to the prophets.

But how terrible for you who are rich now;
you have had your easy life!
How terrible for you who are full now;
you will go hungry!
How terrible for you who laugh now;
you will mourn and weep!
How terrible when all people speak well of you;
their ancestors said the very same things
about the false prophets.

This is the Gospel of the Lord.

>   *All: ~Praise to you, Lord Jesus Christ*

Reflection

* Jesus teaches us "as one who has authority."

* Recall the paradox of Jesus' teaching.

* The happiness that Jesus proclaims is completely contrary to the happiness promised by secular values.

Response

>   *Leader:*   Our help is in the name of the Lord,

>   *All: ~The maker of heaven and earth.*

A Song of Rejoicing   *Revelation 15:3–4*

Antiphon: Let us rejoice in our living and loving God.

Great and amazing are your deeds,
Lord God, the Almighty!
Just and true are your ways,
King of the nations!

Lord, who will not fear
and glorify your name?
For you alone are holy.

All nations will come,
and worship before you,
for your judgments have been revealed.

Glory to you, Source of all being,
Eternal Word, and Holy Spirit:

As it was in the beginning, is now,
and will be for ever. Amen.

Antiphon: Let us rejoice in our living and loving God.

Litany

Leader: Lord Jesus, you are the way, the truth, and the life.

   All: ~*Stand by us, Lord.*

   Lord Jesus, you taught us true happiness.
   ~*Stand by us, Lord.*

   Lord Jesus, you were true to your own teachings.
   ~*Stand by us, Lord.*

   Lord Jesus you were slandered and persecuted
   because you stood for the truth.
   ~*Stand by us, Lord.*

   Lord Jesus, you ask us to be true to our own nature.
   ~*Stand by us, Lord.*

Spontaneous prayers of intercession

Thanksgiving

Leader: Lord, holy Father, almighty and everlasting God,
   we praise and thank you
   for the happiness of the holy Gospel,
   the good news taught by your own dear Son, our Savior.

   We thank you for the gift of our difference,
   for the gift of being special creatures in your sight,
   for the gift of being drawn in love to our own kind.

   We thank you for the profound and prophetic teaching
   that frees us to be ourselves in your sight
   and to look forward to fuller and happier days.

   We thank you for good friends, good books, and movies
   that opened our hearts and our minds
   to our intimate truth.

We thank you for the friendship and support
that cheers and encourages us when we need it most.

Above all, we thank you for the gift
of insight and courage
to come out to ourselves, to our friends,
and even to our enemies.

Send your Holy Spirit into our hearts
with fresh gifts of insight
that we may see our way clear to a new and better life,
to a life of meaning, fellowship
and the service of others.

We praise you, bless you, and thank you,
for you are good and you love our kind,
now and always and for ever and ever.

All: ~Amen.

Blessing

Leader: May the Lord bless us and take care of us.

All: ~Amen.

May the Lord be kind and gracious to us.
~Amen.

May the Lord look on us with favor and + give us peace.
~Amen.

All exchange the kiss of peace with the host and with one another.

ᨀ THE BLESSING OF A HOME

When moving into a new home (apartment, condo, or house), this
blessing service may be used by a single person or couple in a
gathering with their larger family and a group of friends. It is a
renewal and rededication of our common life together and of our
willingness to share our blessings with others.

Leader: In the name of the Father/Mother of us all +
who draws us together by the Word of God
in the unity of the Holy Spirit.

All: ~Amen.

> Peace to this house.
> *~And to all who live here.*

Hymn

Lord, bless our homes with peace and love and laughter,
With understanding and with loyalty.
May we together follow Christ the Master
And know the blessing of his sov'reignty.

May every heart receive his loving spirit
And know the truth that makes life truly free;
Then, in that spirit may we live united,
And find in God our deep security.

Forgive the hurts our selfishness inflicted
On those we love and those who love us best.
Christ, heal the scars, and draw us all together
In God whose will is peace and joy and rest.

— Frank von Christierson (b. 1900)

Psalm 112   THE UPRIGHT DELIGHT IN GOD'S LOVE

Antiphon: A light shines on those who love God.

Blessed are those who fear the Lord,
who greatly delight in God's commandments!
Their descendants will be mighty in the land;
the generation of the upright will be blessed.

Wealth and riches are in their houses,
and their righteousness endures for ever.
They rise in darkness as a light for the upright;
they are gracious, merciful, and righteous.

It is well with those who are generous and lend,
who conduct their affairs with justice.
For the righteous shall never be moved;
they will be remembered for ever.

They are not afraid of evil news;
their hearts are firm, secure in the Lord.

When they see their adversaries,
their hearts are steady, they will not be afraid.

They have distributed freely,
they have given to the poor;
their righteousness endures for ever;
their horn is exalted in honor.

Glory to God, Source of all being,
eternal Word, and Holy Spirit:

as it was in the beginning, is now,
and will be for ever. Amen.

Antiphon: A light shines on those who love God.

Prayer

> *Leader:* Let us pray (*pause for quiet prayer*)
>
> > Lord God of the human family,
> > which you have founded and preserve,
> > make us strong and faithful,
> > hearers of your word and doers of your law.
> > With your loving support,
> > may we cherish one another
> > and be kind to the poor;
> > through Christ Jesus our Lord.
>
> *All:* ~Amen.

First Reading   LOVE ONE ANOTHER   *Ephesians 4:1–6*

I urge you — I who am a prisoner because I serve the Lord: live a life that measures up to the standard God set when he called you. Be always humble, gentle, and patient. Show your love by being tolerant with one another. Do your best to preserve the unity which the Spirit gives by means of the peace that binds you together. There is one body and one Spirit, just as there is one hope to which God has called you. There is one Lord, one faith, one baptism; there is one God and Father of all, who is Lord of all, works through all, and is in all.

Responsory
Ephesians 3:18–19

Leader: May you have the power to understand
how broad and long, how high and deep,
is Christ's love.

All: *~May you have the power to understand how broad and long,
how high and deep, is Christ's love.*

Yes, may you come to know his love.
~How broad and long, how high and deep.

And so be completely filled with the very nature of God.
*~May you have the power to understand how broad and long,
how high and deep, is Christ's love.*

Second Reading   BE MERCIFUL AND FORGIVE   *Luke 6:37–38*

Do not judge others, and God will not judge you; do not condemn
others, and God will not condemn you; forgive others and God will
forgive you. Give to others, and God will give to you. Indeed, you
will receive a full measure, a generous helping, poured into your
hands — all that you can hold. The measure you use for others is
the one that God will use for you.

Reflection

- Moving into a new home is a fresh beginning.

- Love of God and love of neighbor are the greatest
commandments.

- Be humble, gentle, patient, and tolerant toward those we
live with.

Canticle of Revelation
Revelation 15:3–4

Antiphon: Holy is God, holy and strong, holy and living for ever.

Great and amazing are your deeds,
Lord God, the Almighty!
Just and true are your ways,
King of the nations!

Lord, who will not fear
and glorify your name?
For you alone are holy.

All nations will come
and worship before you,
for your judgments have been revealed.

To the King of the ages, immortal invisible,
the only wise God,
be honor and glory, through Jesus Christ,
for ever and ever. Amen.

Antiphon: Holy is God, holy and strong, holy and living for ever.

Litany

> *Leader:* Jesus of the humble home of Nazareth,
>
> *All:* ~*Bless our home.*
>
> Jesus of the wedding feast of Cana,
> ~*Bless our home.*
>
> Jesus of the loaves and fishes,
> ~*Bless our home.*
>
> Jesus of the house of Simon the Pharisee,
> ~*Bless our home.*
>
> Jesus of the home of Martha and Mary,
> ~*Bless our home.*
>
> Jesus of the rich man and Lazarus,
> ~*Bless our home.*
>
> Jesus of the Passover Supper with your disciples,
> ~*Bless our home.*
>
> Jesus of the resurrection meals by the lake of Galilee,
> ~*Bless our home.*
>
> Jesus of the great and final Meal
> at God's welcome table,
> ~*Bless our home.*
>
> *Spontaneous prayers of intercession*

Prayer

Leader: God of hearth and home, of love and laughter,
pour the Spirit of peace and unity into our hearts
and make us love one another as you love us.
Make our home a shrine of your abiding presence,
a place of welcome and rest,
a place of prayer and loving devotion,
a place of hospitality and good cheer.
May Jesus be the silent guest at our table
to bless and encourage us in all our activities
and to guide us onward and upward
to our eternal destiny,
where he lives and reigns with you and the Holy Spirit,
one God, for ever and ever.

All: ~Amen.

Alternative Prayer

Leader: Saving and protecting God,
during the exodus from Egypt,
you protected the homes of the Israelites
from the destroying angel
by the blood of a lamb.
In the same way,
protect us by the blood of the Lamb
who takes away the sins of the world,
and send us an angel from heaven
to visit and defend this home
and all who dwell here;
through the same Christ our Lord.

All: ~Amen.

Blessing

Leader: May the grace of our Lord Jesus Christ
and the love of God, and the fellowship
of the Holy Spirit
+ be with us all.

All: ~Amen.

All may exchange the kiss of peace.

◌ **FOR THE GIFT OF A SPOUSE**

Not every gay or lesbian person has a partner, and not every gay or lesbian person wants a partner. Nevertheless, it seems that the majority of lesbians and gay men long for such a relationship and experience intense loneliness in its absence. Some have had bad experiences of loss or betrayal and feel that they somehow failed to achieve a successful union whether through their own fault, that of others, or both. Such disheartening experiences often leave a residue of fear of failure and even a cynical distrust of other people. One way of overcoming these distrustful feelings is to keep our eyes fixed on the suffering, betrayed, and abandoned Jesus and then take a fresh stand before God, who promised in Christ to hear and help us. Jesus said to his disciples: "Ask, and it will be given you; search, and you will find; knock, and the door will be opened to you" (Matthew 7:7).

This ritual is meant more for private use than for group prayer but may be adapted to the latter.

> *Leader:* Blessed be the name of the Lord,
> \+ the Creator of heaven and earth.
>
> *All:* ~*Amen.*

A Wedding Toast

St. John tells how, at Cana's wedding feast,
The water-pots poured wine in such amount
That by his sober count
There were a hundred gallons at the least.

It made no earthly sense, unless to show
How whatsoever love elects to bless
Brims to a sweet excess
That can without depletion overflow.

Which is to say that what love sees is true;
That the world's fullness is not made but found.
Life hungers to abound
And pour its bounty out for such as you.

Now, if your loves will lend an ear to mine,
I toast you both, good son and dear new lover.
May you not lack for water,
And may that water smack of Cana's wine.

— Richard Wilbur (b. 1921) from *The Mind Reader,*
© 1972, Harcourt, Inc.

Psalm 142   DESERTED BY FRIENDS

Antiphon: You are my refuge,
          my portion in the land of the living.

With my voice I cry to the Lord,
I make my supplication;
before the Lord I tell my trouble,
I pour out my complaint.

When my spirit is faint,
you know my way.
In the path where I walk
they have hidden a trap for me.

Look on my right hand and see;
there is no one who takes notice of me;
no refuge remains for me,
no one cares for me.

I cry to you, O Lord;
I say, "You are my refuge,
my portion in the land of the living."
Give heed to my cry;
for I am brought very low.
Save me from my persecutors;
for they are too strong for me.

Bring me out of prison,
so that I may give thanks to your name!
The righteous will surround me,
for you will deal richly with me.

Antiphon: You are my refuge,
          my portion in the land of the living.

Prayer

Leader: Let us pray (*pause for quiet prayer*)

> Lord Jesus,
> you know what it is like to be betrayed
> or abandoned by friends.
> Listen to my story of distress
> and give me comfort and hope.
> Make me a friend to others
> and give me a friend of my own.
> Blessed be your holy name!

All: ~*Amen.*

Reading   LIVE TOGETHER IN HARMONY   *Romans 15:1–7*

We who are strong ought to put up with the failings of the weak, and not to please ourselves. Each of us must please our neighbor for the good purpose of building up the neighbor. For Christ did not please himself; but, as it is written, "The insults of those who insult you, have fallen on me." For whatsoever was written in former days was written for our instruction, so that by steadfastness and by the encouragement of the scriptures we might have hope. May the God of steadfastness and encouragement grant you to live in harmony with one another, in accordance with Christ Jesus, so that together you may with one voice glorify the God and Father of our Lord Jesus Christ. Welcome one another, therefore, just as Christ has welcomed you, for the glory of God.

Alternative Reading
JUDAS BETRAYS JESUS   *Luke 22:1–6, 47–48, 53*

Now the festival of Unleavened Bread, which is called the Passover, was near. The chief priests and the scribes were looking for a way to put Jesus to death, for they were afraid of the people. Then Satan entered into Judas called Iscariot, who was one of the twelve; he went away and conferred with the chief priests and officers of the temple police how he might betray him to them. They were greatly pleased and agreed to give him money. So he consented and began to look for an opportunity to betray him to them when no crowd was present. . . .

While Jesus was still speaking, suddenly a crowd came, and the one called Judas, one of the twelve, was leading them. He approached Jesus to kiss him; but Jesus said to him, "Judas, is it with a kiss that you are betraying the Son of Man?... But this is your hour, and the power of darkness."

Reflection

- Jesus knew the bitterness of betrayal by Judas, one of his chosen twelve.

- All the rest of his disciples fled and left him alone.

- Simon Peter denied him three times a few hours later.

- Mary his Mother and "the disciple whom Jesus loved" stood loyally at foot of the cross until the bitter end.

Response

Leader: Our help is in the name of the Lord,

All: ~*The maker of heaven and earth.*

Canticle of Tobit

Tobit 13:1–2, 4, 6–7

Antiphon: I extol the Lord, my heart rejoices in God Most High.

Blest be the living God,
reigning for ever,
who strikes, then heals,
casts deep into the grave,
and raises up from utter ruin;
no one eludes God's hand.

Announce God's greatness
wherever you are.
Extol the Lord to everyone:
the Lord is our God,
who fathered us,
God for ever.

When you turn your heart and mind
to live rightly before God,

then God will turn to you
and never hide again.

Match your praise
to all God has done for you.
Bless the Lord of justice,
who rules for ever.

Glory to God: Creator, Redeemer, and Sanctifier:

now and always and for ever and ever. Amen.

Antiphon: I extol the Lord, my heart rejoices
in God Most High.

Litany

   Leader: Lord Jesus, you tell us that we must be born again.

   All: ~*I put my trust in you.*

Lord Jesus, you ask us to leave everything
and follow you.
~*I put my trust in you.*

Lord Jesus, you ask us to bear our own particular cross.
~*I put my trust in you.*

Lord Jesus, you tell us that your words are spirit and life.
~*I put my trust in you.*

Lord Jesus, you feed us with
your own true body and blood.
~*I put my trust in you.*

Lord Jesus you promise to answer our prayers.
~*I put my trust in you.*

Spontaneous prayers of intercession

Prayer

   Leader: Blessed Savior,
you felt deprivation, loneliness,
and abandonment by your sometime friends.
Be my comforter and consoler as you have promised,
make me a friend to others,

and give me one particular friend and companion
on my life's journey.
I praise and thank you in advance for your gifts
and will extol you before my friends for ever.
Blessed be your holy name!

All: ~*Amen.*

Alternative Prayer

Leader: Thank you, Lord Jesus Christ,
for all the benefits and blessing
which you have given me,
for all the pains and insults
you have borne for me.
Merciful Friend, Brother, and Redeemer,
may I know you more clearly,
love you more dearly,
and follow you more nearly,
day by day.

All: ~*Amen.*

— St. Richard of Chichester (1197–1253)

Blessing

Leader: Lord, show your goodness
to those whose hearts are true.

All: ~*Amen.*

⚭ FOR THE GIFT OF A CHILD

Not all gay and lesbian people have children but many do, either
as single parents or as couples. There is also a growing number of
such people adopting children. This ritual gives parents and their
relatives and friends an opportunity to thank God for the birth or
adoption of a child. Soon after the birth or adoption would be a
suitable time to celebrate this thanksgiving.

Leader: In the name of God, the creator and giver of life.

All: ~*Amen.*

Leader: Let us thank the Creator of life for the gift of this child.

Hymn of St. Patrick

Christ be here at either hand,
Christ behind, before me stand,
Christ with me where'er I go,
Christ around, above, below.

Christ be in my heart and mind,
Christ within my soul enshrined,
Christ control my wayward heart,
Christ abide and ne'er depart.

Christ my life and only way,
Christ my lantern night and day,
Christ be my unchanging friend,
Guide and guard me to the end.

— Trans. C. F. Alexander (1818–1895)

Leader: What name do you give this child?

Parents: We call him/her *N*_____ .

Leader: Are you prepared to devote yourselves
to the welfare of this child
during the long years ahead?

Parents: With God's help, we are willing.

Psalm 121   GOD WATCHES, SHIELDS, AND SHELTERS

Antiphon: My help comes from the Lord,
who made heaven and earth.

I lift my eyes to the hills —
from where does my help come?
My help comes from the Lord,
who made heaven and earth.

The Lord will not let your foot be moved,
the Lord who keeps you will not slumber.
The One who keeps Israel
will neither slumber nor sleep.

The Lord is your keeper;
the Lord is your shade
on your right hand.
The sun shall not strike you by day,
nor the moon by night.

The Lord will keep you from all evil,
and will keep your life.
The Lord will keep your going out
and your coming in
from this time forth and for evermore.

Antiphon: My help comes from the Lord,
who made heaven and earth.

Prayer

Leader: Let us pray (*pause for quiet prayer*)

Holy Father, Giver of life,
in heaven you established the serried ranks
of angels and archangels
to celebrate your glory.
As we welcome new life into our family,
may the angels surround and assist us
to serve and glorify your goodness
for all glory, honor, and worship are your due,
now and for ever.

All: ~*Amen.*

First Reading   LITTLE CHILDREN   *Mark 10:13–16*

People were bringing little children to Jesus in order that he might touch them; and the disciples spoke sternly to them. But when Jesus saw this he was indignant and said to them, "Let the little children come to me; do not stop them; for it is to such as these that the kingdom of God belongs. Truly I tell you, whoever does not receive the kingdom of God as a little child will never enter it." And he took them up in his arms, laid his hands on them, and blessed them.

Responsory   *Matthew 18:5, 10, 14*

Leader: Your Father in heaven does not want
        any of these little ones to be lost.

   All: *~Your Father in heaven does not want*
        any of these little ones to be lost.

        Whoever welcomes one such child in my name
        welcomes me.
        ~Your Father in heaven does not want
        any of these little ones to be lost.

        Their angels continually see the face
        of my Father in heaven.
        ~Your Father in heaven does not want
        any of these little ones to be lost.

        Glory to the Father, and to the Son,
        and to the Holy Spirit.
        ~Your Father in heaven does not want
        any of these little ones to be lost.

Second Reading   BECOME LIKE CHILDREN   *Matthew 18:1–5, 10*

The disciples came to Jesus and asked, "Who is greatest in the
kingdom of heaven?" He called a child, whom he put among them,
and said: "Truly I tell you, unless you change and become like
children, you will never enter the kingdom of heaven. Whoever
becomes humble like this child is the greatest in the kingdom of
heaven. Whoever welcomes one such child in my name welcomes
me. . . . Take care that you do not despise one of these little ones;
for, I tell you, in heaven their angels continually see the face of my
Father in heaven."

Reflection by the leader and/or others.

Leader: With the Virgin Mary, the mother of Jesus,
        let us praise and thank God for the gift of *N*_____ .

Song of the Blessed Virgin Mary *Luke 1:46–55*

Antiphon: Blest is the womb that bore you, O Christ,
and the breasts that nursed you!

My soul + proclaims the greatness of the Lord,
My spirit sings to God, my saving God,
Who on this day above all others favored me
And raised me up, a light for all to see.

Through me great deeds will God make manifest,
And all the earth will come to call me blest.
Unbounded love and mercy sure will I proclaim
For all who know and praise God's holy name.

God's mighty arm, protector of the just,
Will guard the weak and raise them from the dust.
But mighty kings will swiftly fall from thrones corrupt,
The strong brought low, the lowly lifted up.

Soon will the poor and hungry of the earth
Be richly blest, be given greater worth.
And Israel, as once foretold to Abraham,
Will live in peace throughout the promised land.

All glory be to God, Creator blest,
To Jesus Christ, God's love made manifest,
And to the Holy Spirit, gentle Comforter,
All glory be, both now and evermore. Amen.

Antiphon: Blest is the womb that bore you, O Christ,
and the breasts that nursed you!

— Text: *Magnificat,* trans. Owen Alstott
© 1993 Oregon Catholic Press

Litany

Leader: For the mystery and blessing of children,

All: ~*We thank you, O Lord.*

For new and abundant life in this child,
~*We thank you, O Lord.*

For the opportunity and challenge of parenting,
~*We thank you, O Lord.*

For the blessing of parents, grandparents,
and other relatives,
~We thank you, O Lord.

For the strength and support of good friends,
~We thank you, O Lord.

For the grace to persevere in our good intentions,
~We thank you, O Lord.

Spontaneous prayers of intercession

Prayer

Leader: Creator of the world and giver of life,
we thank you for the gift of *N*_____ .
Make us worthy and wise to raise *him/her*
with wisdom, understanding, and courage.
Prepare us for the inevitable difficulties ahead
and make us grateful for the challenge.
We offer you our family life
with full confidence that you will never fail us.
May we, in turn, never fail you or this child
but grow together in wisdom and age
before you and our fellow human beings.
Blessed be God for ever!

All: ~Amen.

Alternative Prayer

Leader: Be with us, O Savior of the world,
to shield us from life's major tragedies,
to make us conscious of our responsibilities,
and to bring us to our senses when we fail.
Without you, Lord Jesus, we can do nothing.
Enlarge our hearts to embrace the wider world
beyond our immediate family,
and to share ourselves with others.
Root us in the Good News you announced
and make us thankful for all our blessings.
Blessed be the holy name of Jesus,
now and for ever!

All: *~Amen.*

Blessing

Leader: May the blessing of God,
the creator and sustainer of life,
+ be our strength and our stay.

All: ~*Amen.*

⁓ HOLY BAPTISM

Since there is a growing number of children among gay people,
this ritual may be used by parents, adoptive parents, grandparents,
other relatives, and friends the evening prior to the baptism. It may
also be used to celebrate each anniversary of the child's baptism.

On occasion, gay or lesbian parents may encounter reluctance
from local ministers of the Gospel to baptize their child. If this
reluctance occurs, we must remember that, by universal Christian
consent, any baptized person can administer baptism in the case
of necessity. In such cases, this ritual could serve as an actual baptismal rite with baptism coming just after the recitation of the
Apostles' Creed.

It is customary in some churches to baptize on the Lord's Day a
short period after birth. Adopted children who have not been baptized may be christened shortly after the adoption goes through.
Godparents should be active Christians devoted to the welfare
of the child and prepared to set the child a good example of a
Christian life.

Leader: Blessed be God: Creator, + Redeemer, and Sanctifier.

All: ~*Amen.*

Hymn

Let all the world in ev'ry corner sing:
My God and King!
The heavens are not too high,
His praises there may fly;
The earth is not too low,
His praises there may grow.
Let all the world in ev'ry corner sing:
My God and King!

Let all the world in ev'ry corner sing:
My God and King!
The church with psalms must shout,
No door can keep them out;
But, more than all, the heart
Must bear the longest part.
Let all the world in ev'ry corner sing:
My God and King!

— George Herbert (1593–1633)

Psalm 36:5–13   THE LORD OF LIFE

Antiphon: No one can see the Kingdom of God
without being born again.

Your steadfast love, O Lord, extends to the heavens,
your faithfulness to the clouds.
Your righteousness is like the mighty mountains,
your judgments are like the great deep;
O Lord, you save humans and animals.

O God how precious is your steadfast love!
All people may take refuge in the shadow of your wings.
They feast on the abundance of your house,
and you give them drink from the river of your delights.
O continue your steadfast love to those who know you,
and your salvation to the upright of heart!

Antiphon: No one can see the Kingdom of God
without being born again.

Prayer

Leader: Let us pray (*pause for quiet prayer*)

By your gift, O Lord of life,
we are born again by water and the Holy Spirit,
for you are the fount of life
and in your light we see light.
Make us faithful to the vows of our baptism,
and devoted members of your holy church,
today and every day of our lives.
We ask this through Christ our Lord.

All: ~*Amen.*

First Reading   NEW BIRTH, NEW LIFE   *Titus 3:4–7*

When the kindness and love of God our Savior were revealed, he saved us. It was not because of any good deeds that we ourselves had done, but because of his own mercy that he saved us, through the Holy Spirit, who gives us new birth and new life by washing us. God poured out the Holy Spirit abundantly on us through Jesus Christ our Savior, so that by his grace we might be put right with God and come into possession of the eternal life we hope for.

Responsory   *Matthew 28:18–20*

Leader: Jesus said to his disciples: Go to all peoples everywhere and make them my disciples.

All: *~Jesus said to his disciples: Go to all peoples everywhere and make them my disciples.*

Baptize them in the name of the Father, the Son, and the Holy Spirit.
~And make them my disciples.

Leader: Teach them to obey everything
I have commanded you.
~And make them my disciples.

And I will be with you always, to the end of the age.
~And make them my disciples.

Leader: Glory to the Father, and to the Son,
and to the Holy Spirit.
~Jesus said to his disciples: Go to all peoples everywhere and make them my disciples.

Gospel Reading   THE SUMMARY OF THE GOSPEL   *John 3:14–17*

As Moses lifted up the bronze snake on a pole in the desert, in the same way the Son of Man must be lifted up, so that everyone who believes in him may not die but have eternal life. For God loved the world so much that he gave his only Son, so that everyone who believes in him may not die but have eternal life. For God did not send his Son into the world to be its judge, but to be its savior.

Or This Gospel   JESUS AND CHILDREN   *Mark 10:13–16*

People were bringing little children to Jesus in order that he might touch them; and the disciples spoke sternly to them. But when Jesus saw this, he was indignant and said to them, "Let the little children come to me; do not stop them; for it is to such as these that the kingdom of God belongs. Truly I tell you, whoever does not receive the kingdom of God as a little child will never enter it." And he took them up in his arms, laid his hands on them, and blessed them.

Reflection

- In baptism, God claims us as his own and always stays faithful to us.

- He announces the Good News to us in and by Christ.

- Jesus is not our judge but our Savior.

> *Leader:* Let us recite together the Apostles' Creed,
> our profession of faith and commitment.

I believe in God, the Father almighty,
creator of heaven and earth.

I believe in Jesus Christ, God's only Son, our Lord
who was conceived by the Holy Spirit,
born of the Virgin Mary,
suffered under Pontius Pilate,
was crucified, died, and was buried;
he descended to the dead.
On the third day he rose again;
he ascended into heaven,
he is seated at the right hand of the Father,
and he will come again to judge the living and the dead.

I believe in the Holy Spirit,
the holy catholic church,
the communion of saints,
the forgiveness of sins,
the resurrection of the body,
and the life everlasting. Amen.

Rite of Baptism under Special Circumstances

With the support of two godparents, the Leader immerses the naked child three times in a convenient container of water while reciting the baptismal formula. If the parents prefer, the Leader may baptize by pouring water on the child's head three times while reciting these same baptismal words:

> *Leader:* N⸺, I baptize you in the name of the Father,
> and of the Son, and of the Holy Spirit.

> *All:* ~*Amen.*

The child is then wrapped in her/his baptismal garments and returned to the parents or godparents to hold. The Leader then seals the child with the sign of the cross:

> *Leader:* Child of God,
> receive the sign + of the cross on your forehead
> and never be ashamed of Christ your Savior.

The Leader presents a burning candle to the parents:

> *Leader:* Take this burning candle and let the light of Christ
> shine in your life.

Litany

> *Leader:* Lord and life-giving Spirit,
> who brooded over the waters when first the world began,

> *All:* ~*Make us dead to sin but alive to God.*

> You led your people out of slavery
> through the waters of the Red Sea
> and into freedom through the waters
> of the Jordan.
> ~*Make us dead to sin but alive to God.*

> You overshadowed Mary of Nazareth
> and made her the Mother of Jesus.
> ~*Make us dead to sin but alive to God.*

> You anointed Jesus as Messiah
> as he was baptized by John in the Jordan.
> ~*Make us dead to sin but alive to God.*

You raised Jesus from the grave
and proclaimed him Son of God in all his power.
~*Make us dead to sin but alive to God.*

You appeared in tongues of flame on Pentecost
and touched each person there.
~*Make us dead to sin but alive to God.*

You charge the waters of baptism with power
to give new life.
~*Make us dead to sin but alive to God.*

Spontaneous prayers of intercession

Prayer

Leader: Almighty and everlasting God,
out of pure mercy,
you decreed both the creation
and the renewal of the world.
Be present and active in the sacraments
which you have instituted for our salvation.
Send forth the Spirit of adoption in full measure
on those who are born of water and the Holy Spirit;
may they live under the power of that same Spirit
all the days of their lives.
We ask this through Jesus our blessed Savior.

All: ~*Amen.*

The Lord's Prayer

Leader: Let us pray together as our Savior taught us:

All: Our Father in heaven,
hallowed be your name,
your kingdom come,
your will be done,
on earth as in heaven.
Give us today our daily bread.
Forgive us our sins
as we forgive those who sin against us.
Save us from the time of trial
and deliver us from evil.

> For the kingdom and the power and the glory
> are yours,
> now and for ever. Amen.

Blessing

Leader: May God, the source of grace and peace,
+ be with us all.

All: ~*Amen.*

Beginning with the parents and godparents, all are invited to kiss the child on the forehead in veneration of the indwelling Spirit.

∞ CONFIRMATION

This ritual may be celebrated by parents, godparents, relatives, and friends on the evening prior to a Confirmation or to mark its anniversary.

Leader: Send forth your Spirit, O God,

All: ~*And renew the face of the earth.*

Hymn to the Holy Spirit

O Holy Spirit, by whose breath
Life rises vibrant out of death:
Come to create, renew, inspire;
Come, kindle in our hearts your fire.

You are the seeker's sure resource,
Of burning love the living source.
Protector in the midst of strife,
The giver and the Lord of life.

In you God's energy is shown,
To us your varied gifts made known.
Teach us to speak, teach us to hear;
Yours is the tongue and yours the ear.

Flood our dull senses with your light;
In mutual love our hearts unite.
Your power the whole creation fills;
Confirm our weak, uncertain wills.

From inner strife grant us release;
Turn nations to the ways of peace,
To fuller life your people bring
That as one body we may sing:

Praise to the Father, Christ his Word,
And to the Spirit, God the Lord;
To them all honor, glory be
Both now and in eternity. Amen.

> — Text: *Veni, Creator Spiritus,* 9th century, trans. John Webster
> Grant, *The Hymn Book of the Anglican Church of Canada* (1971),
> #246

Psalm 97:1–6, 9–12   THE GOD OF MAJESTY AND FIRE

Antiphon: I baptize you with water; he will baptize you
              with the Holy Spirit and with fire.

The Lord reigns; let the earth rejoice;
let many coastlands be glad!
Clouds and thick darkness surround the Lord;
righteousness and justice are the foundations of God's throne.

Fire goes before the Lord,
and burns up God's adversaries on every side.
The Lord's lightnings illumine the world;
the earth sees and trembles.

The mountains melt like wax before the Lord,
before the Lord of all the earth.
The heavens proclaim God's righteousness
and all the peoples behold God's glory.

You, Lord, are most high over all the earth;
you are exalted far above all gods.
The Lord loves those who hate evil,
preserves the lives of the faithful,
and delivers them from the hand of the wicked.

Light dawns for the righteous,
and joy for the upright in heart.
Rejoice in the Lord, O you righteous,
and give thanks to God's holy name.

Antiphon: I baptize you with water; he will baptize you
with the Holy Spirit and with fire.

Prayer

Leader: Let us pray (*pause for quiet prayer*)

Heavenly King, Consoler, Spirit of truth,
present in all places and filling all things,
treasury of blessing and giver of life:
come and dwell in us,
cleanse us from every stain of sin,
and save our souls,
O gracious Lord.

All: ~Amen.

First Reading THE POURING FORTH OF THE SPIRIT *Isaiah 44:1–5*

The Lord says, "I am the Lord who created you; from the time you
were born, I have helped you. Do not be afraid; you are my servant,
my chosen people whom I love. I will give water to the thirsty land
and make streams flow on the dry ground. I will pour out my spirit
on your children and my blessing on your descendants. They will
thrive like well-watered grass, like willows by streams of running
water. One by one, people will say, 'I am the Lord's.' They each will
mark the name of the Lord on their arms and call themselves one
of God's people."

Responsory *John 14:25*

Leader: The Holy Spirit, the Paraclete, will teach you all things
and lead you into all truth.

All: ~*The Holy Spirit, the Paraclete, will teach you all things
and lead you into all truth.*

I will give you a new heart and a new mind.
~*And lead you into all truth.*

I will take away your stubborn heart of stone
and give you an obedient heart.
~*And lead you into all truth.*

Glory to the Father, and to the Son,
and to the Holy Spirit.
*~The Holy Spirit, the Paraclete, will teach you all things
and lead you into all truth.*

Second Reading   THE LAYING ON OF HANDS   *Acts 8:14–17*

The apostles in Jerusalem heard that the people of Samaria had
received the word of God, so they sent Peter and John to them.
When they arrived, they prayed for the believers that they might
receive the Holy Spirit. For the Holy Spirit had not come down on
any of them; they had only been baptized in the name of the Lord
Jesus. Then Peter and John placed their hands on them, and they
received the Holy Spirit.

Reflection

- The Holy Spirit is the life-principle in us.

- The Spirit leads us into all truth.

- The Spirit makes us friends of Jesus and obedient children
  of God.

Doxology

Leader: Blessing, honor, thanksgiving and praise,
more than we can utter, more than we can conceive,
be yours, O holy and glorious Trinity,
Source of all being, eternal Word, and Holy Spirit,
by all angels, by all human beings, and by all creatures,
now and always and for ever and ever.

All: *~Amen.*

The Lord's Prayer

Leader: Lord Jesus, teach us to pray:

All: Our Father in heaven,
hallowed be your name,
your kingdom come,
your will be done,
on earth as in heaven.

Give us today our daily bread.
Forgive us our sins
   as we forgive those who sin against us.
Save us from the time of trial
   and deliver us from evil.
For the kingdom and the power and the glory
   are yours,
     now and for ever. Amen.

Blessing

Leader: May the blessing of almighty God,
    who fills our hearts with peace,
    + descend upon us and remain with us for ever.

All: ~*Amen.*

◌ PREPARATION FOR RECONCILIATION/PENANCE

Love of God and love of neighbor are the basic precepts of our religion: hard to understand and even harder to carry out. We all fall short and need to review our lives and loves regularly. Often this can be spiritually affirming when done with the help of an experienced and sympathetic confessor.

Gay people need to pick their confessor carefully. Ask gay friends for a suitable priest or minister, and do not be afraid of rejecting anyone who seems unhelpful or harmful. In cases of doubt, many gay people will have to rely on a lay friend for spiritual assistance.

The following devotion is a *private* preparation for the Sacrament of Reconciliation and not the sacramental act itself. This devotion is especially suitable for Episcopalians, Lutherans, and Roman Catholics, but other churches also have some form of reconciliation rite available to those who request it.

Leader: In the name of God, + the merciful
    and compassionate.

All: ~*Amen.*

Hymn   GOD'S MERCY

There's a wideness in God's mercy
Like the wideness of the sea;
There's a kindness in God's justice
Which is more than liberty.
There is plentiful redemption
In the blood that has been shed;
There is joy for all the members
In the sorrows of the Head.

For the love of God is broader
Than the measures of our mind,
And the heart of the Eternal
Is most wonderfully kind.
If our love were but more simple
We should take him at his word,
And our lives would be thanksgiving
For the goodness of the Lord.

Troubled souls, why will you scatter
Like a crowd of frightened sheep?
Foolish hearts, why will you wander
From a love so true and deep?
There is welcome for the sinner
And more graces for the good;
There is mercy with the Savior,
There is healing in his blood.

> — Frederick W. Faber (1814–1863), alt. *Worship III*
> (Chicago: GIA, 1986), #595

Psalm 51   A PSALM OF REPENTANCE

Antiphon: O God, be merciful to me a sinner!

Have mercy on me, O God,
according to your steadfast love;
according to your abundant mercy
blot out my transgressions.

Wash me thoroughly from my iniquity,
and cleanse me from my sin!
For I know my transgressions,
and my sin is ever before me.

Against you, you only, I have sinned,
and done that which is evil in your sight,
so that you are justified in your sentence
and blameless in your judgment.

Surely, you desire truth in the inward being;
therefore teach me wisdom in my secret heart.
Purge me with hyssop, and I shall be clean;
wash me, and I shall be whiter than snow;

Let me hear with joy and gladness;
let the bones which you have broken rejoice.
Hide your face from my sins,
and blot out all my iniquities.

Create in me a clean heart, O God,
and put a new and right spirit within me.
Cast me not away from your presence,
and take not your holy spirit from me.

Restore to me the joy of your salvation,
and sustain in me a willing spirit.
Then I will teach transgressors your ways,
and sinners will return to you.

Deliver me from bloodshed, O God,
God of my salvation,
and my tongue will sing aloud of your deliverance.
O Lord, open my lips,
and my mouth shall show forth your praise.

For you have no delight in sacrifice;
were I to give a burnt offering,
you would not be pleased.
The sacrifice acceptable to God is a broken spirit;
a broken and contrite heart, O God, you will not despise.

Antiphon: O God, be merciful to me a sinner!

Prayer

Leader: Let us pray (*pause for quiet prayer*)

Lord Jesus Christ,
stretched out between heaven and earth
on the cross for our sins,
and pierced with five grievous wounds:
Reshape my heart after yours
and put a new and willing spirit within me
that I may love and serve you and my neighbor
all the days of my life;
for your own name's sake.

All: ~*Amen.*

An Examination of Conscience

After repentance, this is the most important part of our preparation for acknowledging and confessing our sins. It need not be agonizing but it must be thorough and reflective. Following are a few texts from the Bible to help us reflect on our life and actions before God.

First Reading   *1 John 1:5–10*

This is the message we have heard from him and proclaim to you, that God is light, and in him there is no darkness at all. If we say that we have fellowship with him while we are walking in darkness, we lie and do not do what is true; but if we walk in the light as he himself is in the light, we have fellowship with one another, and the blood of Jesus his Son cleanses us from all sin. If we say that we have no sin, we deceive ourselves, and the truth is not in us. If we confess our sins, he who is faithful and just will forgive us our sins and cleanse us from all unrighteousness. If we say that we have not sinned, we make him a liar, and his word is not in us.

Second Reading   *Romans 13:8–10*

Owe no one anything, except to love one another; for the one who loves another has fulfilled the Law. The commandments, "You shall not commit adultery; You shall not murder; You shall not steal; You shall not covet"; and any other commandment, are summed up in this word, "Love your neighbor as yourself." Love does no wrong to a neighbor; therefore, love is the fulfilling of the Law.

Gospel Reading　　　THE BEATITUDES　　　*Matthew 5:3–10*

Happy are those who know they are spiritually poor;
the kingdom of heaven belongs to them!
Happy are those who mourn;
God will comfort them!
Happy are those who are humble;
they will receive what God has promised!
Happy are those whose greatest desire
is to do what God requires;
God will satisfy them fully!
Happy are those who are merciful to others;
God will be merciful to them!
Happy are the pure in heart;
they will see God!
Happy are those who work for peace;
God will call them his children!
Happy are those who are persecuted
because they do what God requires;
the Kingdom of heaven belongs to them!

Prayer for Repentance and Contrition

God of pardon and peace,
I want to love you
with all my heart and soul and mind
and with all my strength.
Help me to be sorry for my sins
of thought, word, and deed;
for what I have done
and for what I have left undone.
With your help I will change my life
and sin no more in your sight.
In the name of our blessed Savior,
who died on the cross for me,
pardon each and every one of my sins,
and make me a true servant of God
for the rest of my life. Amen.

Prayer before a Crucifix

Good Jesus, friend of all,
I kneel before you hanging on the cross
and recall with sorrow and affection
your five precious wounds,
while I ponder the prophetic words
of King David your ancestor:
"They have pierced my hands and my feet
I can count all my bones" (Psalm 22:17).
Good Jesus, crucified for me,
fix this image of yourself in my heart:
fill me with lively sentiments of faith, hope, and love,
make me truly sorry for my sins
and utterly committed to your Gospel. Amen.

— Text: *En ego, O bone,* 16th century, trans. William G. Storey

Prayer of Self-Dedication to Jesus Christ

Lord Jesus Christ,
take all my freedom,
my memory, my understanding, and my will.
All that I have and cherish
you have given me.
I surrender it all to be guided by your will.
Your grace and your love
are wealth enough for me.
Give me these, Lord Jesus,
and I ask for nothing more.

— St. Ignatius Loyola (ca. 1491–1556), trans. William G. Storey

After a serious preparation, we present ourselves to a minister of reconciliation, confess our sins fully and candidly, listen to the words of counsel and advice, and receive the forgiveness of our sins in a spirit of humility and contrition.

◌ **THE HOLY EUCHARIST**

These devotions may be used at home or in church before receiving
Holy Communion. They may also be used by an individual or by a
group for a First Communion and its anniversary, on the outstand-
ing eucharistic feasts of Holy Thursday and Corpus Christi, or — in
churches that reserve the Sacrament for the communion of the sick
and dying — for devotional visits to the Blessed Sacrament. More
especially, they are helpful for the sick and dying who receive Holy
Communion at home, in a hospital, or in a nursing home. Friends
of the dying and the critically ill may read these prayers with or to
the sick person.

A. PRAYERS FOR HOLY COMMUNION

Hymn

Let all mortal flesh keep silence,
And with awe and trembling stand;
Ponder nothing earthly minded,
For, with blessing in his hand,
Christ our Lord to earth descending,
Our full homage to demand.

King of kings, yet born of Mary,
As of old on earth he stood,
Lord of lords, in human vesture,
In the Body and the Blood,
He will give to all the faithful
His own self for heavenly food.

Rank on rank the host of heaven
Spreads its vanguard on the way,
As the Light of Light descending
From the realms of endless day,
That the powers of hell may vanish
As the darkness clears away.

At his feet the six-winged Seraph,
Cherubim with sleepless eye,

Veil their faces to the Presence,
As with ceaseless voice they cry,
Alleluia! alleluia!
Alleluia! Lord Most High.

> — Text: *Liturgy of St. James,* 5th century,
> trans. Gerard Moultrie (1829–1885)

Prayer before Holy Communion

Almighty and ever-living God,
I approach the sacrament of your only begotten Son,
our Lord Jesus Christ.
I come sick to the doctor of life,
unclean to the fountain of mercy,
blind to the radiance of eternal light,
poor and needy to the Lord of heaven and earth.

Lord, in your great generosity,
heal my sickness, wash away my defilement,
enlighten my blindness, enrich my poverty,
and clothe my nakedness.

May I receive the bread of angels,
the King of kings and Lord of lords,
with humble reverence,
with the purity and faith,
the repentance and love,
and the determined purpose
that will help to bring me to salvation.
May I receive the sacrament
of the Lord's body and blood,
and its reality and power.

Kind God,
may I receive the body of your only begotten Son,
our Lord Jesus Christ,
born from the womb of the Virgin Mary,
and so be received into his mystical body,
and numbered among his members.

Loving Father,
as on my earthly pilgrimage
I now receive your beloved Son

under the veil of a sacrament,
may I one day see him face to face in glory,
who lives and reigns with you for ever. Amen.

> — Attributed to St. Thomas Aquinas (1225–1274),
> *A Book of Prayers* (Washington, D.C.: ICEL, 1982), p. 4

Prayer after Holy Communion

Lord, Father all-powerful, and ever-living God,
I thank you,
for even though I am a sinner,
and your unprofitable servant,
you have fed me
with the precious body and blood
of your Son, our Lord Jesus Christ,
not because of my worth,
but out of your kindness and your mercy.

I pray that this holy communion
may not bring me condemnation and punishment
but forgiveness and salvation.
May it be a helmet of faith
and a shield of good will.
May it purify me from evil ways
and put an end to my evil passions.
May it bring me charity and patience,
humility and obedience,
and growth in the power to do good.

May it be my strong defense
against all my enemies, visible and invisible,
and the perfect calming of all my evil impulses,
bodily and spiritual.
May it unite me more closely to you,
the one true God,
and lead me safely through death
to everlasting happiness with you.

And I pray that you will lead me, a sinner,
to the banquet where you,
with your Son and Holy Spirit,
are true and perfect light,

total fulfillment, everlasting joy,
gladness without end,
and perfect happiness to your saints.
Grant this through Christ our Lord. Amen.

> — Attributed to St. Thomas Aquinas (1225–1274),
> *A Book of Prayers,* p. 9

Anima Christi

Soul of Christ make me holy.
Body of Christ feed me.
Blood of Christ cover me.
Water from Christ's side wash me.
Passion of Christ strengthen me.
O good Jesus hear me.
In your wounds hide me.
From all sin keep me.
From Satan protect me.
At the hour of death call me.
To your side invite me
to praise you with all your saints
for ever and ever. Amen.

> — Text: *Anima Christi,* 14th century,
> trans. William G. Storey

B. DEVOTION TO THE BLESSED SACRAMENT

Leader: I am the living bread of heaven, says the Lord.

All: ~*Anyone who eats this bread will live for ever.*

Eucharistic Hymn

Hail our Savior's glorious Body,
Which his Virgin Mother bore;
Hail the Blood which, shed for sinners,
Did a broken world restore;
Hail the sacrament most holy,
Flesh and Blood of Christ adore!

Come, adore this wondrous presence;
Bow to Christ, the source of grace!
Here is kept the ancient promise

Of God's earthly dwelling place!
Sight is blind before God's glory,
Faith alone may see his face!

Glory be to God the Father,
Praise to his co-equal Son,
Adoration to the Spirit,
Bond of love, in Godhead one!
Blest be God by all creation
Joyously while ages run.

> — Text: *Pange, lingua, gloriosi* by St. Thomas Aquinas (1225–1274), trans. James Quinn, S.J., *Praise for All Seasons* (Kingston, N.Y.: Selah Publishing Co., 1994), p. 59

Psalm 43   PRAISE OF GOD, MY SAVIOR

Antiphon: I will go to the altar of God,
to God, my exceeding joy.

Vindicate me, O God, and defend my cause
against an ungodly people;
from the deceitful and unjust
deliver me!

For you are the God in whom I take refuge;
why have you cast me off?
Why do I mourn because of the oppression
of the enemy?

O send out your light and your truth;
let them lead me,
let them bring me to your holy hill
and to your dwelling!

Then I will go to the altar of God,
to God my exceeding joy;
and I will praise you with the lyre,
O God, my God.

O why am I so burdened,
and why am I so troubled?
Hope in God whom again I shall praise,
my help and my God.

Antiphon: I will go to the altar of God,
to God, my exceeding joy.

Prayer

Leader: Let us pray (*pause for quiet prayer*)

God of mercy and compassion,
send out your light and your truth
through Jesus Christ our Lord.
As we rejoice before the altar of your presence
deliver us from our burdens
and give us the grace to hope in you,
now and for ever.

All: ~*Amen.*

Gospel Reading THE BODY AND BLOOD OF CHRIST *John 6:53–58*

Jesus said to them, "Very truly, I tell you, unless you eat the flesh
of the Son of Man and drink his blood, you have no life in you.
Those who eat my flesh and drink my blood have eternal life, and I
will raise them up on the last day; for my flesh is true food and my
blood is true drink. Those who eat my flesh and drink my blood
abide in me, and I in them. Just as the living Father sent me, and I
live because of the Father, so whoever eats me will live because of
me. This is the bread that came down from heaven, not like that
which your ancestors ate, and they died. But the one who eats this
bread will live for ever."

Reflection

• At the Lord's table we are all united in Christ.

• He provides us with the true and living bread.

• Those who eat and drink as he commanded will live for ever.

Response

Leader: Do not work for the food that perishes,

All: ~*But for the food that endures for eternal life.*

Canticle of the Blessed Virgin Mary   *Luke 1:46–55*

Antiphon: How sacred is the feast
             in which Christ is our food,
             the memorial of his passion is renewed,
             our hearts are filled with grace,
             and we receive a pledge of the glory
             that is to come, alleluia!

My soul + proclaims the greatness of the Lord.
My spirit sings to God, my saving God,
Who on this day above all others favored me
And raised me up, a light for all to see.

Through me great deeds will God make manifest,
And all the earth will come to call me blest.
Unbounded love and mercy sure will I proclaim
For all who know and praise God's holy name.

God's mighty arm, protector of the just,
Will guard the weak and raise them from the dust.
But mighty kings will swiftly fall from thrones corrupt,
The strong brought low, the lowly lifted up.

Soon will the poor and hungry of the earth
Be richly blest, be given greater worth.
And Israel, as once foretold to Abraham,
Will live in peace throughout the promised land.

All glory be to God, Creator blest,
To Jesus Christ, God's love made manifest,
And to the Holy Spirit, gentle Comforter,
All glory be, both now and evermore. Amen.

— Text: *Magnificat,* trans. Owen Alstott,
© 1993 Oregon Catholic Press

Antiphon: How sacred is the feast
             in which Christ is our food,
             the memorial of his passion is renewed,
             our hearts are filled with grace,
             and we receive a pledge of the glory
             that is to come, alleluia!

Litany of the Blessed Sacrament

Leader: Lord, have mercy.

All: ~*Lord, have mercy.*

Christ, have mercy.
~*Christ, have mercy.*

Lord, have mercy.
~*Lord, have mercy.*

Christ, hear us.
~*Christ, graciously hear us.*

God the Father in heaven,
~*Have mercy on us.*

God the Son, Redeemer of the world,
~*Have mercy on us.*

God the Holy Spirit,
~*Have mercy on us.*

Holy Trinity, one God,
~*Have mercy on us.*

Word made flesh and living among us,
~*Christ, have mercy on us.*

Pure and acceptable sacrifice,
~*Christ, have mercy on us.*

Hidden manna from above,
~*Christ, have mercy on us.*

Living bread that came down from heaven,
~*Christ, have mercy on us.*

Bread of life for a hungry world,
~*Christ, have mercy on us.*

Chalice of blessing,
~*Christ, have mercy on us.*

Precious blood that washes away our sins,
~*Christ, have mercy on us.*

Memorial of God's undying love,
~*Christ, have mercy on us.*

Food that lasts for eternal life,
~*Christ, have mercy on us.*

Mystery of faith,
~*Christ, have mercy on us.*

Medicine of immortality,
~*Christ, have mercy on us.*

Food of God's chosen,
~*Christ, have mercy on us.*

Perpetual presence in our tabernacles,
~*Christ, have mercy on us.*

Viaticum of those who die in the Lord,
~*Christ, have mercy on us.*

Pledge of future glory,
~*Christ, have mercy on us.*

Be merciful,
~*Spare us, good Lord.*

Be merciful,
~*Graciously hear us, good Lord.*

By the great longing you had to eat
the Passover with your disciples.
~*Christ, have mercy on us.*

By your humility in washing their feet,
~*Christ, have mercy on us.*

By your loving gift of this divine sacrament,
~*Christ, have mercy on us.*

By the five wounds of your precious body,
~*Christ, have mercy on us.*

By your sacrificial death on the cross,
~*Christ, have mercy on us.*

By the piercing of your sacred heart,
~*Christ, have mercy on us.*

By your glorious resurrection and ascension
into heaven,
~Christ, have mercy on us.

By the gift of the Paraclete Spirit,
~Christ, have mercy on us.

By your return in glory to judge the living
and the dead,
~Christ, have mercy on us.

Lamb of God, you take away the sins of the world,
~Have mercy on us.

Lamb of God, you take away the sins of the world,
~Have mercy on us.

Lamb of God, you take away the sins of the world,
~Grant us your peace.

You gave them bread from heaven to be their food.
~And this bread contained all goodness.

Prayer

Leader: Let us pray *(pause for quiet prayer)*

Lord Jesus Christ,
you gave us the holy Eucharist
as the memorial of your suffering and death.
May our worship of this sacrament
of your body and blood
help us to experience the salvation you won for us
and the peace of the kingdom,
where you live with the Father and the Holy Spirit,
one God, for ever and ever.

All: *~Amen*

— ICEL, *Corpus Christi*

Prayer of Praise

Leader: May the Heart of Jesus
in the most blessed Sacrament
be praised, adored, and loved,
with grateful affection,

at every moment,
in all the tabernacles of the world,
even unto the end of time.

All: ~*Amen.*

⊛ AN ORDER FOR UNITING TWO PEOPLE IN A HOLY UNION

Many gay and lesbian Christians want to celebrate their coming together as a couple in the presence of good friends who understand
and support their commitment. While there are some ministers
who are willing to preside at such ceremonies, there are many ordained ministers who may not or will not officiate. In any event,
Christian couples must note that an ordained minister is only an
official witness on behalf of the church to those who make the
promises or vows. That is the prerogative of the couple themselves!

As a suggestion, the leader of prayer and the two people to be
united could stand facing their friends, behind a table holding a
cross, candle, flowers, and a copy of the Scriptures.

Leader: Blessed be the Reign of God:
Creator, + Redeemer, and Sanctifier,
now and always and for ever and ever.

All: ~*Amen.*

Holy is God, holy and strong,
holy and living for ever.
~*Come, let us adore the living God,*
who made us to love and serve him
in this world, and to enjoy him in the next.

Heavenly King, Consoler, Spirit of truth,
present in all places and filling all things,
treasury of blessings and giver of life:
Come and dwell in us,
cleanse us from every stain of sin,
and save our souls,
O gracious Lord.
~*Amen.*

A Poem   CANA OF GALILEE

Once when our eyes were clean as noon, our rooms
Filled with the joys of Cana's feast:
For Jesus came, and his disciples, and his Mother,
And after them the singers
And some men with violins.

Once when our minds were Galilees,
And clean as skies our faces,
Our simple rooms were charged with sun.
Our thoughts went in and out in whiter coats
than God's disciples',
In Cana's crowded rooms, at Cana's tables.

Nor did we seem to fear the wine would fail:
For ready, in a row, to fill with water and a miracle,
We saw the earthen vessels, waiting empty.
What wine those humble waterjars foretell!

> — Thomas Merton (1915–1968), *Collected Poems of Thomas Merton*
> (New York: New Directions, 1964), Trustees of the Merton
> Legacy Trust

Psalm 133   LOVE AND FRIENDSHIP

Antiphon: Jesus says: "Love one another
             as I have loved you."

Behold, how good and pleasant it is
when kindred live together in unity!

It is like precious oil on the head,
running down the beard,
the beard of Aaron,
running down on the collar of his robes!

It is like the dew of Hermon
which falls on the mountains of Zion!

For there the Lord has commanded the blessing:
Life for ever!

Antiphon: Jesus says: "Love one another
             as I have loved you."

Prayer

Leader: Let us pray (*pause for quiet prayer*)

> Jesus, our teacher and Lord,
> you have commanded us to love one another
> as you have loved us
> and laid down your life for us.
> In your infinite love
> help us by your enabling grace
> to live in love after your sacrificial pattern
> and to be models of faithful devotion.
> For you, O Christ, are the lover of humankind,
> now and for ever.

All: ~*Amen.*

First Reading

THE LOYALTY AND FIDELITY OF RUTH   *Ruth 1:1, 6, 11–17, 22*

In the days when the judges ruled, there was a famine in the land, and a certain man of Bethlehem in Judah went to live in the country of Moab. [After his death and the death of his two sons] Naomi his wife started to return with her daughters-in-law from the country of Moab.... But Naomi said, "Turn back, my daughters, why will you go with me?... Go your way, for I am too old to have a husband. No, my daughters, it has been far more bitter for me than for you, because the hand of the Lord has turned against me." Then they wept aloud again. Orpah kissed her mother-in-law, but Ruth clung to her. So she said, "See, your sister-in-law has gone back to her people and to her gods; return after your sister-in-law." But Ruth said, "Do not press me to leave you or to turn back from following you! Where you go, I will go; where you lodge, I will lodge; your people shall be my people, and your God my God. Where you die, I will die — there will I be buried...." So Naomi returned together with Ruth the Moabite, who came back with her from the country of Moab.

Alternative Reading

THE FRIENDSHIP OF DAVID AND JONATHAN   *1 Sam. 18:1–2 Sam. 1:26*

When David had finished speaking to King Saul, the soul of his son Jonathan was bound to the soul of David, and Jonathan loved him as his own soul. Saul took him that day and would not let him return to his father's house. Then Jonathan made a covenant with David, because he loved him as his own soul. Jonathan stripped himself of the robe that he was wearing, and gave it to David, and his armor, and even his sword and his bow and his belt.... [Later] Saul spoke with his son Jonathan and with all his servants about killing David [out of jealousy]. But Saul's son Jonathan took great delight in David. Jonathan told David, "My father Saul is trying to kill you...." Jonathan spoke well of David to his father Saul...and Saul heeded the voice of Jonathan; Saul swore, "As the Lord lives, he shall not be put to death." So Jonathan called David and related all these things to him. Jonathan then brought David to Saul, and he was in his presence as before....

Jonathan made a covenant with the house of David, saying, "May the Lord seek out the enemies of David." Jonathan made David swear again by his love for him; for he loved him as he loved his own life.

Now the Philistines fought against Israel; and the men of Israel fled before the Philistines, and many fell on Mount Gilboa...and the Philistines killed Jonathan and the [other] sons of Saul.... After the death of Saul, David intoned this lamentation over Saul and his Jonathan:

> "Your glory, O Israel, lies slain upon your high places!
> How the mighty have fallen!
> Saul and Jonathan, beloved and lovely!...
> Jonathan lies slain upon your high places.
> I am distressed for you, my brother Jonathan;
> greatly beloved were you to me;
> your love to me was wonderful,
> passing the love of women."

Responsory   *Sirach 14:20; 15:4–6*

> *Leader:* Happy those who feast on Wisdom
>   and savor her knowledge.
>
> *All:* ~*Happy those who feast on Wisdom*
>   *and savor her knowledge.*
>
>   They will lean on her and not stumble.
>   ~*And savor her knowledge.*

She will raise them above their peers.
~And savor her knowledge.

That their name may always endure.
*~Happy those who feast on Wisdom
and savor her knowledge.*

Gospel Reading
THE DISCIPLE WHOM JESUS LOVED   *John 13:21–26*

Jesus was troubled in spirit, and declared, "Very truly, I tell you, one of you will betray me." The disciples looked at one another, uncertain of whom he was speaking. One of his disciples — the one whom Jesus loved — was reclining next to him; Simon Peter therefore motioned to him to ask Jesus of whom he was speaking. So while reclining next to Jesus, he asked him, "Lord, who is it?" Jesus answered, "It is the one to whom I give this piece of bread when I have dipped it in the dish." So when he had dipped the piece of bread, he gave it to Judas son of Simon Iscariot.

Alternative Gospel   LOVE ONE ANOTHER   *John 15:12–17*

Jesus said to his disciples: "This is my commandment, that you love one another as I have loved you. No one has greater love than this, to lay down one's life for one's friends. You are my friends if you do what I command you. I do not call you servants any longer, because the servant does not know what the master is doing; but I have called you friends, because I have made known to you everything that I have heard from my Father. You did not choose me but I chose you. And I appointed you to go and bear fruit, fruit that will last, so that the Father will give you whatever you ask him in my name. I am giving you these commands so that you may love one another."

Reflections by the leader and/or the group

Act of Commitment

Leader: Friends, we are gathered here to bear witness
to a voluntary act of commitment
by *N*_____ and *N*_____.
Let us stand with them in good times and bad
and support them today and every day.

First Person, facing and holding the hands of the other:

In the presence of God and of these friends,
I, *N*_____ , take you, *N*_____ , for my life partner,
and commit myself to you
in thought, word, and deed.

You are my *brother/sister* in Christ
and I shall treat you
as I would want you to treat me.
So help me God. Amen.

The Second Person makes the same promises.

The Exchange of Rings

First Person: Take this ring, *N*_____ , and wear it
as a sign of my loyalty to you.

Second Person: Take this ring, *N*_____ , and wear it
as a sign of my loyalty to you.

Litany

Leader: In peace, let us pray to the Lord.

All: ~*Lord, hear our prayer.*

For peace from on high
and for the salvation of our souls,
let us pray to the Lord.
~*Lord, hear our prayer.*

For the peace of the whole world
and the union of all,
let us pray to the Lord.
~*Lord, hear our prayer.*

For these your servants, *N*_____ and *N*_____ ,
and their mutual affection, let us pray to the Lord.
~*Lord, hear our prayer.*

For the gifts of perfect love and inseparable union,
let us pray to the Lord.
~*Lord, hear our prayer.*

For the gifts of wisdom and common sense,
let us pray to the Lord.
~*Lord, hear our prayer.*

For a blameless life and pleasing conduct,
let us pray to the Lord.
~*Lord, hear our prayer.*

For all those suffering in mind or body
and for the dying,
let us pray to the Lord.
~*Lord, hear our prayer.*

For refreshment, light, and peace
for the faithful departed,
let us pray to the Lord.
~*Lord, hear our prayer.*

For those who mourn
that their tears be wiped away
by the mystery of the cross,
let us pray to the Lord.
~*Lord, hear our prayer.*

For freedom from all sorrow, pain, anger, and affliction,
let us pray to the Lord.
~*Lord, hear our prayer.*

Help, save, pity, and defend us, O God, by your grace.

Spontaneous prayers of intercession

Leader: Rejoicing in the communion of the Holy Spirit
and of the whole company of heaven,
let us commend ourselves, one another,
and our whole life to Christ our blessed Savior.

All: ~*To you, O Lord.*

Prayer

Leader: Gracious Creator of the human race,
you fashioned us in your own image and likeness
and called us to eternal life in Christ Jesus,
your only Son, our Savior.

In your great pleasure, you joined together in pairs
your holy apostles and martyrs Peter and Paul,
and your glorious martyrs Sergius and Bacchus,
Cosmas and Damian, Perpetua and Felicity,
and Agnes and Cecilia,
uniting them not by the bond of blood
but by the ties of fidelity and loving kindness.

Bless these servants of yours, *N*_____ and *N*_____,
now united as friends and *brothers/sisters*
by faith and mutual devotion.
May they live in peace and harmony
and love and serve one another
all the days of their life together;
through the grace of your Holy Spirit,
and the prayers of all the saints
who pleased you in every generation;
for yours is the kingdom and the power and the glory,
Father, Son, and Holy Spirit, now and for ever.

All: ~*Amen.*

Alternative Prayer

Leader: O God of love and peace,
you commanded us to love and serve one another
and to walk in the footsteps of Jesus,
who freely gave himself for us
and for our salvation.

Look with kindness on *N*_____ and *N*_____,
who want to be your disciples and followers.
Grace them with the love that never ends,
the love that is patient and kind,
that bears all things, believes all things,
hopes all things, endures all things.
We ask this in Jesus' name.

All: ~*Amen.*

The Lord's Prayer

Leader: Let us pray together as Jesus taught us:

All: Our Father in heaven,
hallowed be your name,
your kingdom come,
your will be done,
   on earth as in heaven.
Give us today our daily bread.
Forgive us our sins
   as we forgive those who sin against us.
Save us from the time of trial
   and deliver us from evil.
For the kingdom and the power and the glory
   are yours,
      now and for ever. Amen.

Leader: Lord our God, lover of the human race,
you gathered together your apostles
and all your holy martyrs and saints
into the peace and unity of Christ's church.

Now unite *N*_____ and *N*_____
in a holy kiss of peace and union,
in obedience to your command to love one another.
Grant them undying fidelity to you and to one another
and bring them both at long last to the paradise
where all is peace, love, and joy for evermore.

All: ~*Amen.*

Leader: Let us exchange the kiss of peace
with *N*_____ and *N*_____ .

The couple kiss the Gospels, one another, and then all present.

⚭ FOR BIRTHDAYS

God created us and made us who we are. Birthdays are a fine
occasion for remembering this central fact and for thanking God
for all his gifts of nature and of grace. Surrounded by friends who
support and encourage us, let us rejoice in our sexual orientation

and aspire to make the most of it in the sight of God and of our neighbors.

Leader: Our help + is in the name of the Lord,

    All: ~*The maker of heaven and earth.*

Hymn

O God beyond all praising,
We worship you today
And sing the Lord amazing
That songs cannot repay;
For we can only wonder
At every gift you send,
At blessings without number
And mercies without end:
We lift our hearts before you
And wait upon your word,
We honor and adore you,
Our great and mighty Lord.

Then hear, O gracious Savior,
Accept the love we bring,
That we who know your favor
May serve you as our King;
And whether our tomorrows
Be filled with good or ill,
We'll triumph through our sorrows
And rise to bless you still:
To marvel at your beauty
And glory in your ways,
And make a joyful duty
Our sacrifice of praise.

          — Words: Michel Perry (b. 1942).
        Words © 1982, 1987 by Jubilate Hymns, Ltd.

Psalm 108:1–6   GOD IS UNFAILING LOVE

My heart is steadfast, O God,
my heart is steadfast;
I will sing and make melody.
Awake, my soul!

Awake, O harp and lyre!
I will awake the dawn.

I will give thanks to you, O Lord, among the peoples,
I will sing praises to you among the nations.
For your steadfast love is higher than the heavens,
your faithfulness reaches to the clouds.

Be exalted, O God, above the heavens,
let your glory be over all the earth.
Save with your right hand, and answer me,
so that those whom you love may be rescued.

Prayer

Leader: Let us pray (*pause for quiet prayer*)

Creator God,
you have made us for yourself
and our hearts are restless until they rest in you.
Grace our lives with self-acceptance
and turn our wills toward you
and toward our brothers and sisters
in praise and thanksgiving for the gift of life.
May your glory spread across the earth!

All: ~*Amen.*

Reading SING TO GOD *Colossians 3:16–17*

Let the word of Christ dwell in you richly; teach and admonish
one another in all wisdom; and with gratitude in your hearts sing
psalms, hymns, and spiritual songs to God. And whatever you do,
in word or deed, do everything in the name of the Lord Jesus,
giving thanks to God the Father through him.

Responsory *Psalm 139:13–14*

Leader: You formed my inward parts,
you knit me together in my mother's womb.

All: ~*You formed my inward parts,*
you knit me together in my mother's womb.

I am fearfully and wonderfully made.
~*You knit me together in my mother's womb.*

Wonderful are your works!
~You knit me together in my mother's womb.

Glory to the Father, and to the Son,
and to the Holy Spirit.
~You created every part of me,
you knit me together in my mother's womb.

Second Reading   HUMAN CREATION   *Genesis 1:26–27, 31*

God said, "Let us make humankind in our image, according to our likeness; and let them have dominion over the fish of the sea, and over the birds of the air, and over the cattle, and over all the wild animals of the earth, and over every creeping thing that creeps upon the earth." So God created humankind in his image, in the image of God he created them. . . . God saw everything that he had made, and indeed, it was very good.

Gospel Reading   HUMAN BEINGS   *John 16:21–22*

When a woman is in labor, she has pain, because her hour has come. But when her child is born, she no longer remembers the anguish because of the joy of having brought a human being into the world. So you have pain now; but I will see you again, and your hearts will rejoice, and no one will take your joy from you.

Reflection

- God created only what is good.

- God wants us to be his images on earth.

- Gay and lesbian people are full human beings.

Response

Leader: Our help is in the name of the Lord,

   All: *~The maker of heaven and earth.*

Canticle of the Virgin Mary   *Luke 1:46–55*

Antiphon: Let us make humankind in our image,
              according to our likeness.

My soul + proclaims the greatness of the Lord,
my spirit rejoices in God my Savior,
for you, Lord, have looked with favor on your lowly servant.

From this day all generations will call me blessed:
you, the Almighty, have done great things for me
and holy is your name.
You have mercy on those who fear you,
from generation to generation.

You have shown strength with your arm
and scattered the proud in their conceit,
casting down the mighty from their thrones
and lifting up the lowly.
You have filled the hungry with good things
and sent the rich away empty.

You have come to the aid of your servant Israel,
to remember the promise of mercy,
the promise made to our forebears,
to Abraham and his children for ever.

Glory to the holy and undivided Trinity:

now and always and for ever and ever. Amen.

Antiphon: Let us make humankind in our image,
according to our likeness.

Litany of Praise and Thanksgiving

See pages 213–214

Blessing

> *Leader:* May the grace of our Lord Jesus Christ,
> and the love of God,
> and the communion of the Holy Spirit
> + be with us all.
>
> *All:* ~*Amen.*

○₷ A LAMENT FOR ONE ABANDONED BY FAMILY OR FRIENDS

Many gay and lesbian people have the dispiriting experience of
losing family and friends when they "come out" or are forced to
declare their sexual orientation. Sometimes this loss leads to de-
pression and even despair. Their efforts at living successful lives

are impaired. In the midst of such difficulties, a person needs to experience God's loving care through the help of fellow Christians. This prayer service may be used by individuals or by a group of friends supporting such a person.

> *Leader:* In the name of the Good Shepherd
> + who makes us lie down in green pastures.

> *All:* ~*Amen.*

St. Patrick's Breastplate

Christ be with me, Christ within me,
Christ behind me, Christ before me,
Christ beside me, Christ to win me
Christ to comfort and restore me,

Christ above me, Christ beneath me,
Christ in quiet, Christ in danger,
Christ in the hearts of all that love me,
Christ in the mouth of friend and stranger.

> — Trans. C. F. Alexander (1818–1895)

Psalm 71:1–6, 12–16   A LAMENT OF SOMEONE SHUNNED

Antiphon: My God, my God,
why have you abandoned me?

In you, O Lord, do I take refuge;
let me never be put to shame!
In your righteousness deliver me and rescue me;
listen to me, and save me!

Be to me a rock of refuge,
a strong fortress, to save me,
for you are my rock and my fortress.
Rescue me, O God, from the hand of the wicked,
from the grasp of the unjust and the cruel.

For you, O Lord, are my hope,
my trust, O Lord, from my youth.
Upon you I have leaned from my birth;
it was you who took me from my mother's womb.
My praise is continually of you.

O God, be not far from me;
O my God, make haste to help me!
Let my accusers be put to shame and consumed;
let those who seek to hurt me
be covered with scorn and disgrace.

But I will hope continually,
and I will praise you yet more and more.
My mouth will tell of your righteous acts,
of your deeds of salvation all day long,
for their number is past my knowledge.
I will come praising the mighty deeds of the Lord God,
I will praise your righteousness, yours alone.

Antiphon: My God, my God,
        why have you abandoned me?

Prayer

Leader: Let us pray (*pause for quiet prayer*)

        God my protector and helper,
        when my family and friends desert me,
        you stand by me always.
        Be my rock and my haven,
        as I trust in your desire to free me
        from depression and despair,
        so that I may rejoice in praising you
        through Jesus, my loving Savior.

All: ~Amen.

Gospel Reading

RENOUNCING ALL FOR JESUS' SAKE   *Matthew 8:19–22*

A scribe approached Jesus and said, "Teacher, I will follow you
wherever you go." And Jesus said to him, "Foxes have holes, and
birds of the air have nests; but the Son Man has nowhere to lay
his head." Another of his disciples said to him, "Lord, first let me
go and bury my father." But Jesus said to him, "Follow me, and
let the dead bury their own dead."

Gospel Reading   JESUS AND HIS FAMILY   *Matthew 12:46–50*

While Jesus was still speaking to the crowds, his mother and his brothers were standing outside, wanting to speak to him. Someone told him, "Look, your mother and your brothers are standing outside, wanting to speak to you." But to the one who had told him this, Jesus replied, "Who is my mother, and who are my brothers?" And pointing to his disciples, he said, "Here are my mother and my brothers! For whoever does the will of my Father in heaven is my brother and sister and mother."

Reflection

- Even Jesus was not always understood by his family.

- Apparently his closest relatives were upset with him because he rocked the boat.

- Many in his hometown of Nazareth scoffed at him and rejected him.

- No disciple is above his Master!

Response

Leader: O God, come to my assistance.

All: ~*O Lord, make haste to help me.*

Canticle of Hannah   *1 Samuel 2:1–4, 7, 8*

Antiphon: God pulls down tyrants from their thrones,
        and raises up the lowly.

My heart exults in the Lord,
my strength is exalted in my God.
There is none holy like the Lord,
there is none beside you,
no rock like our God.

For you, O Lord, are a God of knowledge
and by you our actions are weighed.
The bows of the mighty are broken
but the feeble gird on strength.

You, Lord, kill and bring to life;
bring down to Sheol and raise up again.

You, Lord, make poor and make rich;
you bring low and you also exalt.

You raise up the poor from the dust
and lift the needy from the ash-heap
to make them sit with princes
and inherit a seat of honor.

For yours, O Lord, are the pillars of the earth,
and on them you have set the world.

Glory to God, Source of all being,
eternal Word, and Holy Spirit:

as it was in the beginning, is now,
and will be for ever. Amen.

Antiphon: God pulls down tyrants from their thrones,
and raises up the lowly.

Litany of the Holy Name of Jesus

See pages 208–210

Prayer

Leader: Maker of heaven and earth,
protector of those who love you,
guard and keep us from all the obstacles
which the world, the flesh, and the devil,
— and even our family and friends —
put in our path to tempt and discourage us.
We ask this in Jesus' name.

All: ~Amen.

Blessing

Leader: May the glorious passion of our Lord Jesus Christ
+ bring us to the joys of paradise.

All: ~Amen.

⊙ FOR OUR ENEMIES IN HIGH PLACES

Matthew Shepard, we remember you
and your barbed-wire crucifixion!

One of the frustrating facts gay and lesbian people have to confront constantly is that numerous people in society and, sadly, in places of authority are prejudiced against people with a homosexual orientation. Such people not only demean and insult gay and lesbian people, but often attack their lifestyle by hindering how gay and lesbian people live their lives and earn a living. Consequently, the affective lives of gay and lesbian people are ridiculed and threatened by bullies, who feel at liberty to resort to physical violence.

There are two things that can be done to alleviate this distress in the face of such harmful attitudes. First, stare hatred in the face and label it for what it is. In the Scriptures, there are supportive texts that help us recognize our enemies, label them, and pray for deliverance (e.g., Matthew 15:1–20). Second, try to understand and forgive such distressing behavior. Matching hatred with hatred will only make you like them! Say the Lord's Prayer in all earnestness, knowing that you will be forgiven only to the degree that you forgive.

The following ritual may be used in time of distress or when an action of prejudice is experienced or remembered by an individual or a group.

> *Leader:* In the name of the God of justice and mercy
> and of the Last Judgment!

> *All:* ~*Amen.*

Hymn

"Forgive our sins as we forgive,"
You taught us, Lord, to pray,
But you alone can grant us grace
To live the words we say.

How can your pardon reach and bless
The unforgiving heart
That broods on wrongs and will not let
Old bitterness depart?

In blazing light your Cross reveals
The truth we dimly knew:
What trivial debts are owed to us,
How great our debt to you!

Lord, cleanse the depths within our souls
And bid resentment cease.
Then, bound to all in bonds of love,
Our lives will spread your peace.

> — Rosamund Herklots (b. 1905)
> © Oxford University Press

Psalm 109:1–5, 21–22, 26–31
WE DEMAND GOD'S INTERVENTION

Antiphon: Let them curse, O Lord,
but you will bless.

Do not be silent, O God of my praise,
for wicked and deceitful mouths are opened against me,
speaking against me with lying tongues.

They surround me with words of hate,
and attack me without cause.
In return for my love they accuse me,
even while I make prayer for them.
So they reward me evil for good,
and hatred for my love.

But you, O Lord my Lord,
act on my behalf for your name's sake;
because your steadfast love is good,
deliver me.
For I am poor and needy,
and my heart is pierced within me.

Help me, O Lord my God!
Save me according to your steadfast love.
Let them know that this is your hand;
you, O Lord, have done it.

May my accusers be clothed with dishonor;
may they be wrapped in their own shame as in a robe.
With my mouth I will give great thanks to the Lord;

I will praise God in the midst of a throng.
For God stands at the right hand of the needy,
to save them from those who condemn them to death.

Antiphon: Let them curse, O Lord,
but you will bless.

Prayer

Leader: Let us pray (*pause for quiet prayer*)

Just and merciful God,
do not stand silent
in the face of my accusers.
Be true to your name,
show mercy and rescue me
from those who know no mercy;
We ask this through Jesus,
Lord of the living and the dead.

All: ~*Amen.*

First Reading LEAVE ROOM FOR GOD'S WRATH *Romans 12:14–21*

Bless those who persecute you; bless and do not curse them. Rejoice with those who rejoice, weep with those who weep. Live in
harmony with one another; do not be haughty, but associate with
the lowly; do not claim to be wiser than you are. Do not repay
anyone evil for evil, but take thought for what is noble in the sight
of all. If it is possible, so far as it depends on you, live peaceably
with all. Beloved, never avenge yourselves, but leave room for the
wrath of God; for it is written, "Vengeance is mine, I will repay,
says the Lord." No, if your enemies are hungry, feed them; if they
are thirsty, give them something to drink; for by doing this you will
heap burning coals on their heads. Do not be overcome by evil, but
overcome evil by good.

Responsory   *Jeremiah 17:7*

Leader: They are blest who trust in God.

All: ~*They are blest who trust in God.*

Who trust in the Lord alone.
They are blest who trust in God.

They are like trees near a stream.
They are blest who trust in God.

Stretching their roots to water.
They are blest who trust in God.

Glory to the Father, and to the Son,
and to the Holy Spirit
They are blest who trust in God.

Gospel Reading A HARD SAYING *Matthew 5:43–48*

Jesus taught them, saying: "You have heard that it was said, 'You shall love your neighbor and hate your enemy.' But I say to you, Love your enemies, and pray for those who persecute you, so that you may be children of your Father in heaven; for he makes his sun rise on the evil and on the good, and sends rain on the righteous and the unrighteous. For if you love those who love you, what reward do you have? Do not even tax collectors do the same? And if you greet only your brothers and sisters, what more are you doing than others? Do not even the Gentiles do the same? Be perfect, therefore, as your heavenly Father is perfect."

Reflection

- Jesus calls us to the perfection of the Gospel.

- We are forgiven if we forgive others.

- We must not avenge ourselves but leave it up to God.

Lamentation of Jeremiah *Lamentations 5:1–21*

Antiphon: Why have you forgotten us, O Lord,
forsaken us these many days?

Remember, O Lord, what has befallen us;
look and see our disgrace!
Our inheritance has been turned over to strangers,
our homes to aliens.

We have become orphans, fatherless;
our mothers are like widows.
We must pay for the water we drink;
the wood we get must be bought....

The joy of our hearts has ceased;
our dancing has been turned to mourning.
The crown has fallen from our head.
Because of this our hearts are sick,
because of these things our eyes have grown dim. . . .

But you, O Lord, reign for ever;
your throne endures to all generations.
Why have you forgotten us completely?
Why have you forsaken us these many days?

Restore us to yourself, O Lord,
that we may be restored;
renew our days as of old.

Glory to God: Creator, Redeemer, and Sanctifier:

Now and always and for ever and ever. Amen.

Antiphon: Why have you forgotten us, O Lord,
forsaken us these many days?

The Lord's Prayer

Leader: Lord, teach us to pray.

All: ~Our Father in heaven,
hallowed be your name,
your kingdom come,
your will be done,
   on earth as in heaven.
Give us today our daily bread.
Forgive us our sins
   as we forgive those who sin against us.
Save us from the time of trial
   and deliver us from evil.
For the kingdom and the power and the glory
   are yours,
      now and for ever. Amen.

Blessing

Leader: May the God of justice, mercy, and compassion
+ guide and guard us all the days of our life.

All: ~*Amen.*

◌ **AT VARIANCE WITH ONE'S FAMILY**

Because they were mature and brave enough to come out to their families, many lesbian and gay people have experienced bitterness, rejection, and even violence from those who had once cherished them. The homophobia of family members is a particularly cruel affront to one's dignity and self-possession.

Like Jesus, who took his destined path and was misunderstood by his own brothers and sisters, we can expect a certain amount of the same fate. It is part of our prophetic mission to prepare the way of the Lord who wants to set us free both from our own fears and from the fears and disdain of our families. Being his disciple is both a challenge and an opportunity: a challenge to our courage and persistence and an opportunity to testify to the truth of our nature as we see and experience it.

> *Leader:* In the name of the One
>   + who loves and preserves us.
>
>   *All:* ~Amen.

Hymn

The head that once was crowned with thorns
Is crowned with glory now;
A royal diadem adorns
The mighty Victor's brow.

The highest place that heaven affords
Belongs to him by right;
The King of kings and Lord of lords,
And heaven's eternal Light.

The joy of all who dwell above,
The joy of all below,
To whom he manifests his love,
And grants his name to know.

To them the cross with all its shame,
With all its grace, is given;
Their name an everlasting name;
Their joy the joy of heaven.

They suffer with their Lord below;
They reign with him above;
Their profit and their joy to know
The mystery of his love.

The cross he bore is life and health,
Though shame and death to him,
His people's hope, his people's wealth,
Their everlasting theme.

— Thomas Kelly (1769–1855), *The Book of Hymns,* ed. Ian Bradley
(Woodstock, N.Y.: Overlook Press, 1989), p. 409

Psalm 86:1–13   YOU ALONE ARE TRUSTWORTHY

Antiphon: Turn to me, O Lord, and be gracious.

Hear, O Lord, and answer me,
for I am poor and needy.
Preserve my life, for I am devoted to you;
save your servant who trusts in you.

You are my God;
be gracious to me, O Lord,
for I cry to you all day long.
Gladden the life of your servant
for I lift up my life to you, O Lord.

For you, O Lord, are good and forgiving,
abounding in steadfast love to all who call on you.
O Lord, hear my prayer;
listen to my cry of supplication.

In the day of my trouble I call on you,
for you will answer me.
There is none like you among the gods, O Lord,
nor are there any works like yours.

All the nations you have made shall come
and bow down before you, O Lord,
and shall glorify your name.
For you are great and do wondrous things,
you alone are God.

Teach me your way, O Lord,
that I may walk in your truth;
give me an undivided heart
to revere your name.

I will give you thanks, O Lord my God, with my whole heart,
and I will glorify your name for ever.
For great is your steadfast love toward me;
you have delivered my life from the depths of Sheol.

Antiphon: Turn to me, O Lord, and be gracious.

Prayer

Leader: Let us pray (*pause for quiet prayer*)

God of mercy and caring,
when I feel abandoned or despised
show me a sign of your love.
Your dear Son suffered from misunderstanding
from those who did not know what they were doing.
Help me to forgive those who insult or taunt me
for the way you have made me.
Bring me help and comfort,
in the name of Jesus, our loving Savior.

All: ~Amen.

Gospel Reading

ENEMIES IN ONE'S HOUSEHOLD   *Matthew 10:32–39*

Everyone who acknowledges me before others, I also will acknowl-
edge before my Father in heaven; but whoever denies me before
others, I will also deny before my Father in heaven. Do not think
that I have come to bring peace to the earth; I have not come to
bring peace, but a sword. For I have come to set a man against his
father, and a daughter against her mother, and a daughter-in-law
against her mother-in-law; and one's foes will be members of one's
own household. Whoever loves father and mother more than me
is not worthy of me; and whoever loves son or daughter more than
me is not worthy of me; and whoever does not take up the cross
and follow me is not worthy of me. Those who find their life will
lose it, and those who lose their life for my sake will find it.

Reflection

- Jesus experienced the pain of rejection by his relatives.

- Peace at all costs is not the way of the Christian.

- The sword of division both separates and unites.

Responsory

Leader: Blessed are those who mourn,

   All: *~For they will be comforted.*

Canticle of St. Peter the Apostle   *1 Peter 2:21–24*

Antiphon: By his wounds you have been healed.

Christ suffered for you,
leaving you an example,
so that you should follow in his footsteps.

He committed no sin,
and no deceit was found in his mouth.

When he was abused,
he did not return abuse;
when he suffered,
he did not threaten;
but he entrusted himself
to the one who judges justly.

He himself bore our sins
in his body on the cross,
so that, free from sins,
we might live for righteousness;
by his wounds you have been healed.

Glory to God, Source of all being,
eternal Word, and Holy Spirit:

As it was in the beginning, is now,
and will be for ever. Amen.

Antiphon: By his wounds you have been healed.

The Lord's Prayer

Leader: Let us pray as Jesus taught us.

All: Our Father in heaven,
hallowed be your name,
your kingdom come,
your will be done,
   on earth as in heaven.
Give us today our daily bread.
Forgive us our sins
   as we forgive those who sin against us.
Save us from the time of trial
   and deliver us from evil.
For the kingdom and the power and the glory
   are yours,
   now and for ever. Amen.

Prayer

Leader: Lord Jesus,
in Nazareth, your hometown,
you experienced the loss of friends and fellow citizens
when you walked the road laid out for you by God.
Even your family took offense at you,
questioned your sanity,
and tried to restrain you.
By your example and with your aid,
help us both to stand amazed
at the ignorance and misunderstanding of our families
and to embrace them despite their behavior.
Be our strength in our hour of need,
for your own name's sake.

All: ~Amen.

Blessing

Leader: May Jesus, our guide and example,
+ bless us and keep us in our time of trial.

All: ~Amen.

❧ IN TIME OF TEMPTATION

Jesus was sorely tempted by the Devil at the beginning of his public life (Matthew 4:1–11), and toward the end of it felt almost overwhelmed by grief and fear in the Garden of Gethsemane (Luke 22:39–46). He prayed to be delivered, and God sent him the help he needed to survive and carry on his mission. From time to time we all have special moments of temptation that try our courage and steadfastness. Like Jesus we have the right to appeal to God for a clear mind and for strength to do the right thing.

Leader: In the name of God + who rescues and renews us.

All: ~Amen.

Hymn

This world, my God, is held within your hand,
Though we forget your love and steadfast might
And in the changing day uncertain stand,
Disturbed by morning, and afraid of night.

From youthful confidence to careful age,
Help us each one to be your loving friend,
Rewarded by the faithful servant's wage,
God in Three Persons, reigning without end.

— Hamish Swanston, © 1971, Faber Music Ltd.

Psalm 77:1–16　　GOD WILL RESCUE ONCE MORE

Antiphon: Wake up and pray;
　　　　　do not give in to temptation.

I cry aloud to God,
aloud to God, that God may hear me.

In the day of my trouble I seek the Lord;
in the night my hand is stretched out continually;
my life refuses to be comforted.
I think of God, and I moan;
I meditate, and my spirit faints.

You keep my eyelids from closing;
I am so troubled that I cannot speak.

I consider the days of old,
I remember the years long ago.
I commune with my heart in the night;
I meditate and search my spirit.

Will the Lord spurn for ever
and never again be favorable?
Has God's steadfast love ceased for ever?
Are God's promises at an end for all time?
Has God forgotten to be gracious?
Has God's anger shut up compassion?

I will call to mind the deeds of the Lord;
I will remember your wonders of old.
I will meditate on all your work,
and muse on your mighty deeds.

Your way, O God, is holy.
What god is great like our God?
You are the God who works wonders,
you manifested your might among the peoples.
With your arm you redeemed your people,
the descendants of Jacob and Joseph.

Antiphon: Wake up and pray;
do not give in to temptation.

Prayer

Leader: Let us pray (*pause for quiet prayer*)

God of mercy and compassion,
come and help me in my hour of need.
You sent angels to Jesus to give him strength;
reach out and save me too
and keep me among your loyal children,
now and for ever.

All: ~Amen.

First Reading   GOD'S GRACE RESCUES US   *Romans 7:21–25*

I find it to be a law that when I want to do what is good, evil lies
close at hand. For I delight in the law of God in my inmost self, but
I see in my members another law at war with the law of my mind,

making me captive to the law of sin that dwells in my members. Wretched man that I am! Who will rescue me from this body of death? Thanks be to God through Jesus Christ our Lord!

Alternative Reading   A SPIRIT OF ADOPTION   *Romans 8:14–17*

All who are led by the Spirit of God are children of God. For you did not receive a spirit of slavery to fall back into fear, but you have received a spirit of adoption. When we cry, "Abba, Father!" it is that very Spirit bearing witness with our spirit that we are children of God, and if children, then heirs, heirs of God and joint heirs with Christ — if, in fact, we suffer with him so that we may also be glorified with him.

Reflection

- Abba, our dear Father, wants us to grow up and become real adults.

- Trial and temptation are our lot in life.

- By the grace of God we overcome them and grow.

Response

Leader: Our help is in the name of the Lord,

All: ~*The maker of heaven and earth.*

A Pauline Canticle   *Philippians 2:6–11*

Antiphon: Let the same mind be in you
              that was in Christ Jesus.

Though he was in the form of God,
Jesus did not regard equality with God
as something to be exploited,
but emptied himself,
taking the form of a slave,
being born in human likeness.

And being found in human form,
he humbled himself
and became obedient to the point of death —
even death on a cross.

Therefore God also highly exalted him
and gave him the name
that is above every name,

So that at the name of Jesus
every knee should bend,
in heaven and on earth,
and under the earth,
and every tongue should confess
that Jesus Christ is Lord,
to the glory of God the Father.

To the King of the ages, immortal, invisible,
the only wise God,

be honor and glory, through Jesus Christ,
for ever and ever. Amen.

Antiphon: Let the same mind be in you
that was in Christ Jesus.

Prayer

Leader: God of our life,
there are days when the burdens we carry
chafe our shoulders and weigh us down;
when the road seems dreary and endless,
the skies gray and threatening;
when our lives have no music in them,
and our hearts are lonely,
and our souls have lost their courage.
Flood the path with light,
turn our eyes to where the skies are full of promise;
tune our hearts to brave music;
give us a sense of comradeship
with the heroes and saints of every age;
and so quicken our spirits
that we may be able to encourage
all who travel with us on the road of life,
to your honor and glory.

All: ~*Amen.*

Alternative Prayer

Leader: Dear and gracious Father,
you are the creative origin of all that I am
and of all I am called to be.
With the talents and opportunities I have,
how may I serve you best?
Please guide my mind and heart,
open me to the needs of my country
and of the world,
and help me to choose wisely and practically
for your honor and glory
and for the good of all those whose lives I touch.
In Jesus' name.

All: ~Amen.

Blessing

Leader: Let us bless the holy and undivided Trinity;

All: ~Let us praise and glorify God for ever.

Leader: May the blessing of almighty God, +
the Father, the Son, and the Holy Spirit,
descend upon us and remain with us for ever.

All: ~Amen.

ᘑ FOR DELIVERANCE FROM ADDICTION

Like other people under great stress, many lesbians and gay men become addicted to alcohol or other drugs as they try to relieve their pain. Such addiction is a form of slavery that ruins our lives and seriously affects other people who love and depend on us. In order to shake off the chains of addiction we need all the help we can get. God calls us in Christ to the freedom of the children of God. When we admit that we are addicts and turn to our blessed Savior for help, we can be sure that we are heard and rescued by his power. The friendship of other addicts who have experienced God's power to save us from ourselves is also essential to our struggle toward freedom. An experienced confessor who understands addiction can also be of great assistance.

Leader: Our help + is in the name of the Lord.

All: ~*The maker of heaven and earth.*

Hymn

O Sacred Head surrounded
By crown of piercing thorn,
O bleeding head so wounded
Reviled and put to scorn:

Our sins have marred the glory
Of your most holy face,
Yet angel hosts adore you
And tremble as they gaze.

The Lord of every nation
Was hung upon a tree;
His death was our salvation,
Our sins, his agony.

O Jesus, by your passion,
Your life in us increase;
Your death for us did fashion
Our pardon and our peace.

> — *Salve caput cruentatum,* attributed to St. Bernard of Clairvaux
> (1090–1153), trans. Sir Henry Baker (1821–1877) and
> Melvin L. Farrell, S.S. (b. 1930), © World Library Publications,
> 1961

Psalm 62:1–2, 7–12   TRUE SECURITY IN GOD ALONE

Antiphon: God alone is my rock and my salvation.

In silence I wait for God alone,
from whom my salvation comes.
God alone is my rock and my salvation,
my fortress; I shall never be shaken.

On God rests my deliverance and my honor;
my mighty rock, my refuge is God.
Trust in God at all times, O people;
pour out your heart before God
who is our refuge.

Those of low estate are but a breath,
those of high estate are but a delusion;
in the balance they go up;
they are together lighter than a breath.

Once God has spoken,
twice I have heard this:
power belongs to God;
and to you belong steadfast love, O Lord,
for you repay all according to their work.

Antiphon: God alone is my rock and my salvation.

Prayer

> *Leader:*   Let us pray (*pause for quiet prayer*)

> > Holy and immortal God,
> > you alone make us secure.
> > You know our weakness
> > and our fear of falling.
> > Come to our assistance,
> > fill our hearts with fresh courage,
> > and give us strength and love to persevere.
> > In Jesus' name.

> *All:*   *~Amen.*

First Reading   INNER STRENGTH   *Ephesians 3:14–19*

I bow my knees before the Father, from whom every family in
heaven and on earth takes its name. I pray that, according to the
riches of his glory, he may grant that you may be strengthened in
your inner being with power through his Spirit, and that Christ
may dwell in your hearts through faith, as you are being rooted
and grounded in love. I pray that you may have the power to com-
prehend, with all the saints, what is the breadth and length and
height and depth, and to know the love of Christ that surpasses
knowledge, so that you may be filled with all the fullness of God.

Alternative Reading
FILLED WITH THE SPIRIT   *Ephesians 5:1–2, 15–20*

Be imitators of God, as beloved children, and live in love, as Christ
loved us and gave himself up for us, a fragrant offering and sacrifice

to God. . . . Be careful, then, how you live, not as unwise people but as wise, making the most of the time, because the days are evil. So do not be foolish, but understand what the will of the Lord is. Do not get drunk with wine, for that is debauchery; but be filled with the Spirit, as you sing psalms and hymns and spiritual songs among yourselves, singing and making melody to the Lord in your hearts, giving thanks to God the Father at all times and for everything in the name of our Lord Jesus Christ.

Response   *Galatians 6:14*

> *Leader:* God forbid that I should glory except in the cross
> of our Lord Jesus Christ.
>
> *All:* *~Through the cross the world is crucified to me*
> *and I to the world.*

Gospel Reading   THE CROSS   *Luke 9:22–27*

The Son of Man must undergo great suffering, and be rejected by the elders, chief priests, and scribes, and be killed, and on the third day be raised. Then Jesus said to them all, "If any want to become my followers, let them deny themselves and take up their cross daily and follow me. For those who want to save their life will lose it, and those who lose their life for my sake will save it. What does it profit them if they gain the whole world, but lose or forfeit themselves? Those who are ashamed of me and of my words, of them the Son of Man will be ashamed when he comes in his glory and the glory of the Father and of the holy angels. But truly I tell you, there are some standing here who will not taste death before they see the kingdom of God.

Reflection

- Jesus had to bear the cross of temptation and humiliation.
- The disciple is not above his teacher.
- God rescues those who put their trust in our Savior.

Response

> *Leader:* For freedom Christ has set us free.
>
> *All:* *~Do not submit again to the yoke of slavery.*

Canticle of Revelation   *Revelation 15:3–4*

Antiphon: You alone are holy, O God.

Great and amazing are your deeds,
Lord God the Almighty!
Just and true are your ways,
King of the nations!

Lord, who will not fear
and glorify your name?
For you alone are holy.

All nations will come
and worship before you,
for your judgments have been revealed.

Glory to God, Source of all being,
eternal Word, and Holy Spirit:

as it was in the beginning, is now,
and will be for ever. Amen.

Antiphon: You alone are holy, O God.

Litany   *Psalm 57:1–2, 10–11*

Leader: Be merciful to me, O God, be merciful to me,

All: *~For in you I take refuge.*

In the shadow of your wings I take refuge,
~Till the storms of destruction pass by.

I cry to God Most High,
~To God who shields me.

For your steadfast love is vast as the heavens,
~Your faithfulness extends to the clouds.

Be exalted, O God, above the heavens!
~Let your glory be over all the earth!

Spontaneous prayers of intercession

Prayer

Leader: Lord Jesus,
             you bore the cross of pain and humiliation
             for our sake.
             By the power of this holy cross,
             lift our eyes to the five precious wounds
             of your torn and lacerated body,
             our pledge of life and peace
             and our road to glory,
             O Savior of the world,
             living and reigning with the Father
             and the Holy Spirit,
             now and for ever.

All: ~*Amen.*

Gaelic Blessing

Leader: Deep peace of the running wave to us,
             Deep peace of the flowing air to us,
             Deep peace of the quiet earth to us,
             Deep peace of the shining stars to us,
             Deep peace of the gentle night to us,
             Moon and stars pour their healing light on us,
             Deep peace of Christ the light of the world to us.

All: ~*Amen.*

◌ IN TIME OF DESPAIR

Sometimes the pains and disappointments of life simply overwhelm
us. We feel crushed, defeated, demoralized, shattered. When this
happens, we cry out to God blindly, hoping and despairing in turns,
but knowing that God hears our groans and complaints. When no
one else will listen, God will!

Leader: O God, + come to my assistance.

All: ~*O Lord, make haste to help me.*

Poem

Go to dark Gethsemane,
You that feel the tempter's power;
Your Redeemer's conflict see;
Watch with him one bitter hour;
Turn not from his griefs away;
Learn of Jesus Christ to pray.

Follow to the judgment-hall,
View the Lord of life arraigned;
O the wormwood and the gall!
O the pangs his soul sustained!
Shun not suffering, shame or loss;
Learn of him to bear the cross.

Calvary's mournful mountain climb;
There adoring at his feet,
Mark that miracle of time,
God's own sacrifice complete;
"It is finished!" hear the cry;
Learn of Jesus Christ to die.

Early hasten to the tomb
Where they laid his breathless clay;
All is solitude and gloom.
Who has taken him away?
Christ is risen! he meets our eyes.
Savior, teach us so to rise.

> — James Montgomery (1771–1854), in Bert Polman et al.,
> *Amazing Grace* (Louisville: Westminster/John Knox Press,
> 1994), p. 116

Psalm 77:2–16   GOD SEEMS ABSENT OR EVEN POWERLESS

Antiphon: My God, my God, why have you forsaken me?

I cry aloud to God,
aloud to God, that God may hear me.

In the day of my trouble I seek the Lord;
in the night my hand is stretched out continually;
my life refuses to be comforted.

I think of God, and I moan;
I meditate, and my spirit faints.

You keep my eyelids from closing;
I am so troubled that I cannot speak.
I consider the days of old,
I remember the years long ago.
I commune with my heart in the night;
I meditate and search my spirit.

Will the Lord spurn for ever
and never again be favorable?
Has God's steadfast love ceased for ever?
Are God's promises at an end for all time?
Has God forgotten to be gracious?
Has God's anger shut up compassion?

I will call to mind the deeds of the Lord;
I will remember your wonders of old.
I will meditate on all your work,
and muse on your mighty deeds.

Your way, O God, is holy.
What god is great like our God?
You are the God who works wonders,
you manifested your might among the peoples.
With your arm you redeemed your people,
the descendants of Jacob and Joseph.

Antiphon: My God, my God, why have you forsaken me?

Prayer

> *Leader:* Let us pray (*pause for quiet prayer*)

>> Listening God,
>> you know the secret of our hearts
>> and sound the depths of our being.
>> Even Jesus cried out to you in fear
>> and asked to be delivered from his fate,
>> and yet he said: Your will, not mine!
>> As we shudder before the cross
>> of our misery and despair,
>> keep our eyes fixed on Jesus

and how he mastered sin and death
and smashed the gates of hell.
In Jesus' name, we ask it.

All: ~*Amen.*

Gospel Reading   ASK OUR DEAR FATHER   *Luke 11:11–13*

Is there anyone among you who, if your child asks for a fish, will give a snake instead of a fish? Or if the child asks for an egg, will give a scorpion? If you then, you who are evil, know how to give good gifts to your children, how much more will the heavenly Father give the Holy Spirit to those who ask him?

Alternative Gospel Reading   PRAY ALWAYS   *Luke 18:1–8*

Jesus told them a parable about their need to pray always and not to lose heart. He said: "In a certain city there was a judge who neither feared God nor had respect for people. In that city there was a widow who kept coming to him and saying, 'Grant me justice against my opponent.' For a while he refused; but later he said to himself, 'Though I have no fear of God and no respect for anyone, yet because this widow keeps bothering me, I will grant her justice, so that she may not wear me out by continually coming.'" And the Lord said, "Listen to what the unjust judge says. And will not God grant justice to his chosen ones who cry to him day and night? Will he delay long in helping them? I tell you, he will quickly grant justice to them. And yet, when the Son of Man comes, will he find faith on earth?"

Reflection

- God wants us to trust him completely and not lose heart.

- God is infinitely better than our human parents.

- We need the Holy Spirit to put new confidence in us.

Response

Leader: I place all my trust in you, O Lord;

All: ~*You are my only comforter.*

Canticle

Antiphon: Blessed are they who mourn,
for they shall be comforted.

Blessed are those who trust in the Lord,
whose trust is the Lord.
They shall be like a tree planted by water,
sending out its roots by the stream.

It shall not fear when heat comes,
and its leaves shall stay green;
in the year of drought it is not anxious,
and it does not cease to bear fruit.

Glory to the Father, and to the Son,
and to the Holy Spirit:

as it was in the beginning, is now,
and will be for ever. Amen.

Antiphon: Blessed are they who mourn,
for they shall be comforted.

Litany

Leader: Like travelers lost in a parched and burning desert,

All: ~*We cry unto you, O Lord.*

Like those shipwrecked on a lonely coast,
~*We cry unto you, O Lord.*

Like a mother robbed of a crust of bread
that she was bringing to her starving children,
~*We cry unto you, O Lord.*

Like a prisoner confined to a dank and gloomy dungeon,
~*We cry unto you, O Lord.*

Like a slave torn by his master's lash,
~*We cry unto you, O Lord.*

Like an innocent person led to execution,
~*We cry unto you, O Lord.*

Like all the nations of the earth
before their deliverance dawned,
~*We cry unto you, O Lord.*

Like Christ on the cross when he said:
"My God, my God, why have you forsaken me?"
~*We cry unto you, O Lord.*

Spontaneous prayers of intercession

Prayer

Leader: Lord Jesus, by your cross
we are saved from all sin and sorrow.
Protect us who take refuge
beneath the wings of your cross
and bathe us in the precious blood and water
that gushed from your pierced heart,
O Savior of the world,
living and reigning for ever and ever.

All: ~*Amen.*

Blessing

Leader: The Lord bless us and keep us;
the Lord make his face to shine upon us,
and be gracious to us;
the Lord lift up his countenance upon us,
+ and give us peace.

All: ~*Amen.*

⟨ THANKSGIVING FOR VICTORY

When we are troubled and feel almost overcome by harsh circumstances, we can come to doubt God's care for us or even God's very existence. When relief comes and better times return, it is too easy to forget to thank God for the victory. Thanking God will build our hope and confidence in the future and give us renewed strength to face what happens to us. It will also help us beware of the pride of the Pharisee and cherish the humility of the tax collector (Luke 11:9–14).

Leader: In the name of God: Creator, + Redeemer, and Sanctifier.

All: ~*Amen.*

Hymn

I know that my Redeemer lives;
What joy the blest assurance gives!
He lives, he lives, who once was dead;
He lives, my everlasting Head.

He lives, to bless me with his love;
He lives, to plead for me above;
He lives, my hungry soul to feed;
He lives, to help in time of need.

He lives, and grants me daily breath;
He lives, and I shall conquer death;
He lives, my mansion to prepare;
He lives to bring me safely there.

He lives, all glory to his name;
He lives, my Savior, still the same;
What joy the blest assurance gives;
I know that my Redeemer lives!

> — Samuel Medley (1738–1799) from *Worship III*
> (Chicago: GIA, 1986), #445

Psalm 18:30–33, 35
DAVID'S SONG AFTER GOD RESCUED HIM FROM HIS ENEMIES

Antiphon: You light my lamp, O Lord;
my God lights up my darkness.

The way of God is perfect;
the word of the Lord is tested;
it is a shield for all who take refuge in the Lord.

For who is God except the Lord?
And who is a rock besides our God? —
the God who girded me with strength,
made my way safe,
made my feet like the deer's
and set me secure on the heights.

You have given me the shield of salvation,
and your right hand supported me;
your help has made me great.

Antiphon: You light my lamp, O Lord;
my God lights up my darkness.

Prayer

Leader: Let us pray (*pause for quiet prayer*)

Lord Jesus, you are the light of the world,
the shield of all who seek refuge,
and the rock on which we can build.
Thank you for your support
and for your strengthening Spirit.
Blessed be the name of Jesus!

All: ~*Amen.*

Reading GIVE THANKS *Ephesians 5:19–20*

Fill yourselves with the Spirit. Recite among yourselves psalms and
hymns and inspired canticles, singing and giving praise to the Lord
with all your heart. Give thanks to God the Father everywhere and
for every gift in the name of our Lord Jesus Christ.

Gospel Reading

THE PHARISEE AND THE TAX COLLECTOR *Luke 11:9–14*

Jesus told this parable to some who trusted in themselves that
they were righteous and regarded others with contempt. "Two men
went up to the temple to pray, one a Pharisee and the other a
tax collector. The Pharisee, standing by himself, was praying thus,
'God I thank you that I am not like other people: thieves, rogues,
adulterers, or even like this tax collector. I fast twice a week; I give
a tenth of all my income.' But the tax collector, standing far off,
would not even look up to heaven, but was beating his breast and
saying, 'God be merciful to me, a sinner!' I tell you, this man went
down to his home justified rather than the other; for all who exalt
themselves will be humbled, but all who humble themselves will
be exalted."

Alternative Gospel Reading   ALL FOR GOD   *Luke 18:28–30*

Peter said to Jesus, "Look, we have left our homes and followed you." And he said to them, "Truly I tell you, there is no one who has left house or wife or brothers or parents or children, for the sake of the kingdom of God, who will not get back very much more in this age, and in the age to come eternal life."

Reflection

• Humble recognition of our own sinfulness is simple honesty.

• Pride in the face of God is simple stupidity.

• Sacrifice for the sake of the kingdom of God is our calling.

Response

Leader: We constantly give thanks to God

All: ~*For saving us through Christ.*

Canticle of King David   *1 Chronicles 29:10–13*

Antiphon: Let us praise God,
             the source of all blessings.

Blessed are you, O Lord,
the God of our ancestor Israel,
for ever and ever.
Yours, O Lord, are the greatness,
the power, the glory, the victory,
and the majesty.

For all that is in the heavens
and on the earth is yours;
yours is the kingdom, O Lord,
and you are exalted as head above all.

Riches and honor come from you,
and you rule over all.
In your hand are power and might;
and it is in your hand to make great
and to give strength to all.

And now, our God, we give thanks to you
and praise your glorious name.

To the King of the ages, immortal, invisible,
the only wise God,

be honor and glory, through Jesus Christ,
for ever and ever. Amen.

Antiphon: Let us praise God, the source of all blessings.

Thanksgiving

Leader: It is right and fitting to sing to you,
         to glorify you, to thank you, and to worship you,
         at all times and in all places,
         for you are the God of our ancestors in the faith
         and are always true to your promises.
         You brought us into being from sheer nothingness,
         you raised us up when we had fallen low,
         and never cease to do all in your power to save us
         and draw us into your coming kingdom.
         Grateful praise to you, O God, now and for ever.

All: ~Amen.

Blessing

Leader: May almighty God,
         Creator, Redeemer, and Inspirer,
         + bless us and keep us.

All: ~Amen.

◎ IN TIME OF SERIOUS SICKNESS – I

The visitation of the sick and dying is one of the oldest and most helpful of Christian services. Even when the sick person is unable to respond vocally to our prayers, we need to continue saying them slowly and in a clear voice, especially when a dying person enters into his or her final agony. Since many dying people frequently fall in and out of consciousness, assisting friends should not neglect repeating these or other prayers as often as the need arises. Selected passages from the Bible may also be read aloud to the sick or dying, and especially the last chapters of the four

Gospels on the passion, death, burial, and resurrection of Jesus: Matthew 26–28; Mark 11–16; Luke 22–24; John 11–21. These passages will inspire repentance, hope, and trust and ward off fear and terror.

> *Leader:* In the name of Jesus, + who healed the sick
> and raised the dead.

> *All:* ~Amen.

Poem

God be in my head
  and in my understanding.
God be in my eyes
  and in my looking,
God be in my mouth
  and in my speaking,
God be in my heart
  and in my thinking,
God be at my end
  and at my departing.

— Sarum Prymer, 1514, trans. William G. Storey

Psalm 23   OUR GOOD SHEPHERD

Antiphon: O Savior of the world,
      by your cross and precious blood,
      save us and help us, we humbly pray.

The Lord is my shepherd, I shall not want;
the Lord makes me lie down in green pastures,
leads me beside still waters;
restores my life,
leads me in right paths
for the sake of the Lord's name.

Even though I walk through the darkest valley,
I fear no evil;
for you are with me;
your rod and your staff,
they comfort me.

You prepare a table before me
in the presence of my enemies;
you anoint my head with oil,
my cup overflows.

Only goodness and mercy shall follow me
all the days of my life;
and I shall dwell in the house of the Lord
as long as I live.

Antiphon: O Savior of the world,
by your cross and precious blood,
save us and help us, we humbly pray.

Prayer

Leader: Let us pray (*pause for quiet prayer*)

Good Shepherd of your people,
refresh us with the waters of the Spirit
and lead us to the sweet repose of eternity;
may our comfort be the staff
that flourished in the house of Aaron
and that blossomed
in the house of David of the Virgin Mary;
anoint our heads with the oil of healing
and feed us with the bread and wine from your table
that we may dwell in your house for ever and ever.

All: ~Amen.

Reading   LIFE AND LIGHT   *Job 33:15–28*

In a dream in the vision of the night, when deep sleep falls on
mortals, while they slumber on their beds, then God opens their
ears, and terrifies them with warnings, that he may turn them
aside from their deeds, and keep them from pride, to spare their
souls from the Pit, their lives from traversing the River. They are
also chastened with pain upon their beds, and with continual strife
in their bones, so that their lives loathe bread, and their appetites
dainty food. Their flesh is so wasted away that it cannot be seen;
and their bones, once invisible, now stick out. Their souls draw
near the Pit and their lives to those who bring death. Then, if
there should be for one of them an angel, a mediator, one of a

thousand, one who declares a person upright, and he is gracious to that person, and says, "Deliver him from going down into the Pit; I have found a ransom; let his flesh become fresh with youth; let him return to the days of his youthful vigor." Then he prays to God and is accepted by him, he comes into his presence with joy, and God repays him for his righteousness. That person sings to others and says, "I sinned and perverted what was right, and it was not paid back to me. He has redeemed my soul from going down to the Pit, and my life shall see the light."

Alternative Reading   PERSEVERANCE   *Hebrews 12:1–4*

Since we are surrounded by so great a cloud of witnesses, let us also lay aside every weight and the sin that clings so closely, and let us run with perseverance the race that is set before us, looking to Jesus the pioneer and perfecter of our faith, who for the sake of the joy that was set before him endured the cross, disregarding its shame, and has taken his seat at the right hand of the throne of God. Consider him who endured such hostility against himself from sinners, so that you may not grow weary or lose heart. In your struggle against sin you have not yet resisted to the point of shedding your blood.

Gospel Reading
THE NARROW GATE   *Matthew 7:13–14, 21, 24–27*

The Lord Jesus says: "Enter through the narrow gate; for the gate is wide and the road is easy that leads to destruction, and there are many who take it. For the gate is narrow and the road is hard that leads to life, and there are few who find it.... Not everyone who says to me, 'Lord, Lord,' will enter the kingdom of heaven, but only the one who does the will of my Father in heaven.... Everyone then who hears these words of mine and acts on them will be like a wise man who built his house on rock. The rain fell, the floods came, and the winds blew and beat on that house; but it did not fall, because it had been founded on rock. And everyone who hears these words of mine and does not act on them will be like a foolish man who built his house on sand. The rain fell, and the floods came, and the winds blew and beat against that house, and it fell — and great was its fall!"

Reflection

- Jesus warns us to stick to the straight and narrow path leading to life eternal.

- We must call him "Lord" *and* walk in his footsteps.

- He awaits us at the end of the road; let us persevere!

Response

Leader: The Lord is my light and my salvation;

    All: ~*Whom shall I fear?*

Canticle of Azaria   *Daniel 3:26–27, 29–30, 33–34*

Antiphon: Jesus is the Lamb of God
         who takes away the sins of the world.

Blessed are you, O Lord,
God of our ancestors,
and worthy of praise;
and glorious is your name for ever!

For you are just in all you have done
all your works are true and your ways right,
and all your judgments are true.

For we have sinned and broken your law
in turning away from you;
in all matters we have sinned grievously.

We have not obeyed your commandments,
we have not kept them
or done what you have commanded us
for our own good.

For your name's sake
do not give us up for ever,
and do not annul your covenant.
Do not withdraw your mercy from us,
for the sake of Abraham your beloved
and for the sake of your servant Isaac
and Israel your holy one.

Glory to God: Source of all being,
eternal Word, and Holy Spirit:

as it was in the beginning, is now,
and will be for ever. Amen.

Antiphon: Jesus is the Lamb of God
who takes away the sins of the world.

Litany for the Sick or Dying

Leader: God the Father in heaven,

All: *~Have mercy on us.*

God the Son, Redeemer of the world,
~Have mercy on us.

God the Holy Spirit, our comforter and guide,
~Have mercy on us.

Holy Trinity, one blessed God,
~Have mercy on us.

From all evil and sin,
~Good Lord, deliver us.

From the assaults of the devil,
~Good Lord, deliver us.

From the fear of damnation,
~Good Lord, deliver us.

In the hour of death,
~Good Lord, deliver us.

On the day of judgment,
~Good Lord, deliver us.

By your holy incarnation and virgin birth,
~Good Lord, deliver us.

By your holy cross and bitter passion,
~Good Lord, deliver us.

By your blessed death and burial,
~Good Lord, deliver us.

By your glorious resurrection
and admirable ascension,
~*Good Lord, deliver us.*

By your gift of the Holy Spirit,
~*Good Lord, deliver us.*

By your awesome coming again at the end of time,
~*Good Lord, deliver us.*

By your infinite mercy,
~*Good Lord, deliver us.*

Lamb of God, you take away the sins of the world,
~*Have mercy on us.*

Lamb of God, you take away the sins of the world,
~*Have mercy on us.*

Lamb of God, you take away the sins of the world,
~*Grant us your peace.*

Prayer

Leader: Let us pray (*pause for special petitions*)

Father of mercy and compassion,
you made us in your own image
and your Son died for us on the cross.
Help us to pray at all times,
to be truly sorry for our sins,
and to put our entire trust in you
as we pass from this world to your waiting arms.
In Jesus' name, we pray.

All: ~*Amen.*

Dedication

Leader: Jesus, Mary, and Joseph,

All: ~*I give you my heart and my soul.*

Jesus, Mary, and Joseph,
~*Assist me in my hour of death.*

Jesus, Mary, and Joseph,
~*May I die and rest in peace with you.*

◯ **IN TIME OF SERIOUS SICKNESS – II**

This devotion may be used in preparation for the Anointing of the Sick or Dying or at any time of serious illness.

Leader: In the name of God, + the Lord of life and death.

　　All: ~*Amen.*

Poem　　EASTER LIGHT

Because upon the first glad Easter day
The stone that sealed his tomb was rolled away,
So, through the deepening shadows of death's night,
We see an open door — beyond it, light.

> — Ida N. Munson from *Christ in Poetry,* ed. Thomas C. Clark and
> Hazel D. Clark (New York: Association Press, 1952), p. 218

Psalm 31:9–11, 17, 18, 20, 23, 24　　GRACIOUS GOD

Antiphon: Lord God of truth, into your hands
　　　　　　I commend my spirit.

Be gracious to me, O Lord,
for I am in distress;
my eye is wasted from grief,
my soul and body also.

For my life is spent in sorrow,
and my years with sighing;
my strength fails because of my misery,
and my bones waste away.

Let your face shine on your servant;
save me through your steadfast love!
Do not let me be put to shame, O Lord,
for I call on you.

O how abundant is your goodness,
which you have laid up for those who fear you,
and accomplished for those who take refuge in you,
in the sight of everyone.

Love the Lord, all you godly ones.
The Lord preserves the faithful.

Be strong, and let your heart take courage,
all you who wait for the Lord.

Antiphon: Lord God of truth, into your hands
I commend my spirit.

Prayer

Leader: Let us pray (*pause for quiet prayer*)

Father of all mercies,
you love life and hate death,
and want to help those who suffer
and are consumed by pain and grief.
Lord of life, have pity on us,
and especially on your servant, *N*_____ ,
who puts *her/his* trust in your constant love.
We ask this through Christ our Lord.

All: ~*Amen.*

First Reading   ANOINTING OF THE SICK   *James 5:13–16*

Are any among you suffering? They should pray. Are any cheerful?
They should sing songs of praise. Are any among you sick? They
should call for the elders of the church and have them pray over
them, anointing them with oil in the name of the Lord. The prayer
of faith will save the sick, and the Lord will raise them up; and
anyone who has committed sins will be forgiven. Therefore confess
your sins to one another, and pray for one another, so that you may
be healed. The prayer of the righteous is powerful and effective.

Responsory   *Psalm 31:20, 15*

Leader: How rich your goodness to those who revere you!

All: ~*How rich your goodness to those who revere you!*

Whoever seeks your help finds how lavish you are.
~*How rich your goodness to those who revere you!*

You are my God, my life is in your hands.
~*How rich your goodness to those who revere you!*

Glory to God: Creator, Redeemer, and Sanctifier.
~*How rich your goodness to those who revere you!*

Gospel Reading

CHRIST THE HEALER OF ALL ILLS   *Matthew 15:29–31*

Jesus left there and went along by Lake Galilee. He climbed a hill and sat down. Large crowds came to him, bringing with them the lame, the blind, the crippled, the dumb, and many other sick people, whom they placed at Jesus' feet; and he healed them. The people were amazed as they saw the dumb speaking, the crippled made whole, the lame walking, and the blind seeing; and they praised the God of Israel.

Reflection

- Jesus fed the hungry and healed the sick.

- Jesus asks us to put full trust in him.

- Jesus makes us whole, body and soul.

Litany

Leader: Lord Jesus, Son of David and Son of God,

All: ~*Heal and save us.*

Lord Jesus, you went about preaching the Good News
and curing all kinds of sickness and disease,
~*Heal and save us.*

Lord Jesus, you raised to life the daughter of Jairus,
the only son of the widow of Naim,
and Lazarus whom you loved,
~*Heal and save us.*

Lord Jesus, you cured Simon Peter's
mother-in-law of a fever
and the woman who suffered from hemorrhages,
~*Heal and save us.*

Lord Jesus, you delivered the Gadarene demoniac
and the tormented daughter of the Canaanite woman,
~*Heal and save us.*

Lord Jesus, you cured the Roman officer's
paralyzed servant and the dumb epileptic boy,
~*Heal and save us.*

Lord Jesus, you restored the sight of Bartimaeus,
the blind beggar of Jericho,
and purified many lepers,
~*Heal and save us.*

Lord Jesus, you cured the man with the withered hand
and made cripples whole again,
~*Heal and save us.*

Lord Jesus, you commanded your disciples
to lay hands on the sick
and to anoint them with oil to cure them,
~*Heal and save us.*

Lord Jesus, you continue to work
in the Sacrament of Anointing,
~*Heal and save us.*

Spontaneous prayers of intercession

Doxology

Leader: Let us bless the Father through the Son
and in the Holy Spirit.

All: ~*Blessed be God for ever!*

Leader: Abba, dear Father,
God of all consolation,
it is our duty and our salvation
to praise and thank you at all times and in all places
for healing the souls and bodies of those
who put their trust in you.
Mindful of our Savior's words and deeds
as he went about doing good,
we ask you to heal your servant, *N*_____,
of the illness that afflicts *her/him.*
In your mercy, rid *him/her* of all pain of body and mind,
and restore *her/him* to good health
so that *he/she* may serve you faithfully
in your holy church,
now and for ever and ever.

All: ~*Amen.*

The Lord's Prayer

Leader: Lord Jesus, teach us to pray:

All: ~Our Father in heaven,
hallowed be your name,
your kingdom come,
your will be done,
    on earth as in heaven.
Give us today our daily bread.
Forgive us our sins
    as we forgive those who sin against us.
Save us from the time of trial
    and deliver us from evil.
For the kingdom and the power and the glory
    are yours,
        now and for ever. Amen.

Blessing

Leader: The prayer of faith will save the sick,

All: ~*And the Lord will raise them up again.*

Leader: May Jesus, our merciful Lord and Savior,
who went about doing good,
+ be kind and merciful to us.

All: ~*Amen.*

In addition to the above, the litanies on pp. 205–216 are helpful for assisting the sick and dying. At the last moments we should repeat the holy name of Jesus over and over again with or for the dying person until we are sure death has actually occurred.

◌ FOR A HAPPY DEATH

As life draws to a close because of serious illness or old age, we pray for the grace of a happy death fortified by the sacraments of the church and by the presence and prayers of our friends.

Leader: In the name of Christ, + our resurrection
and our life!

All: ~*Amen.*

Poem

I see his blood upon the rose
And in the stars the glory of his eyes,
His body gleams amid eternal snows,
His tears fall from the skies.

I see his face in every flower;
The thunder and the singing of the birds
Are but his voice — and carven by his power
Rocks are his written words.

All pathways by his feet are worn,
His strong heart stirs the ever-beating sea,
His crown of thorns is twined with every thorn,
His cross is every tree.

> — Joseph Mary Plunkett (d. 1916), from *Christ in Poetry,* ed.
> Thomas C. Clark and Hazel D. Clark (New York: Association
> Press, 1952), p. 256

Psalm 13   IN SUFFERING, RELY ON GOD

Antiphon: Lighten my eyes, O Lord,
            lest I sleep the sleep of death.

How long, O Lord? Will you forget me for ever?
How long must I bear pain in my soul,
and have sorrow in my heart all the day?
How long shall my enemy be exalted over me?

Consider and answer me, O Lord my God;
lighten my eyes, lest I sleep the sleep of death;
lest my enemy say, "I have prevailed;"
lest my foes rejoice because I am shaken.

But I trusted in your steadfast love;
my heart shall rejoice in your salvation.
I will sing to the Lord,
for the Lord has dealt richly with me.

Antiphon: Lighten my eyes O Lord,
            lest I sleep the sleep of death.

Prayer

Leader: Let us pray (*pause for quiet prayer*)

God of loving kindness,
as life in this world draws to a close for us,
we look forward to life everlasting with you
by the grace of Jesus our Savior.
Refresh our souls at the hour of death,
cleanse us of all stain of sin,
and bring us into your presence
by the hands of the holy angels.
Blessed be God, now and for ever!

All: ~*Amen.*

First Reading   GOD'S JUDGMENT SEAT   *Romans 14:7–13*

We do not live to ourselves, and we do not die to ourselves. If we
live, we live to the Lord, and if we die, we die to the Lord; so then,
whether we live or whether we die, we are the Lord's. For we will
all stand before the judgment seat of God. For it is written, "As I
live, says the Lord, every knee shall bow to me and every tongue
shall give praise to God" (Isaiah 45:23). So then, each of us will be
accountable to God. Let us therefore no longer pass judgment on
one another, but resolve instead never to put a stumbling block or
hindrance in the way of another.

Responsory   *Psalm 31:6, 8*

Leader: Lord God of truth,
into your hands I commend my spirit.

All: ~*Lord God of truth, into your hands I commend my spirit.*

For you have redeemed me.
~*Lord God of truth, into your hands I commend my spirit.*

I will rejoice and be glad in your steadfast love.
~*Lord God of truth, into your hands I commend my spirit.*

Glory to the Father, and to the Son,
and to the Holy Spirit.
~*Lord God of truth, into your hands I commend my spirit.*

Gospel Reading   THE NARROW GATE   *Matthew 7:13–14, 24–27*

Jesus said to his disciples: "Enter through the narrow gate; for the gate is wide and the road is easy that leads to destruction, and there are many who take it. For the gate is narrow and the road is hard that leads to life, and there are few who find it.... Everyone who hears these words of mine and acts on them will be like a wise man who built his house on rock. The rain fell, the floods came, and the winds blew and beat on that house, but it did not fall, because it had been founded on rock. And everyone who hears these words of mine and does not act on them will be like a foolish man who built his house on sand. The rain fell, and the floods came, and the winds blew and beat against that house, and it fell — and great was its fall!"

Reflection

- We shall all stand naked before the judgment seat.
- Each of us will be accountable to God.
- We shall be very glad if we have built our lives on the rock that is Christ, our Lord and Savior.

Response

Leader: Even though I walk through the darkest valley

    All: ~I fear no evil for you are with me.

Canticle of St. Peter the Apostle   *Peter 2:21–24*

Antiphon: Blessed be the name of Jesus,
          our Lord and Savior!

Christ suffered for you,
leaving you an example,
so that you should follow in his steps.

He committed no sin,
and no deceit was found in his mouth.

When he was abused,
he did not return abuse;
when he suffered,
he did not threaten;

but he entrusted himself
to the One who judges justly.

He himself bore our sins
in his body on the cross,
so that, free from sins,
we might live for righteousness;
by his wounds you have been healed.

Antiphon: Blessed be the name of Jesus,
          our Lord and Savior!

Litany

Leader: Lord Jesus, image of the God we cannot see,

All: *~Be with us at the hour of our death.*

Lord Jesus, who existed before time began,
~Be with us at the hour of our death.

Lord Jesus, through whom the universe was made,
~Be with us at the hour of our death.

Lord Jesus, head of your body, the church,
~Be with us at the hour of our death.

Lord Jesus, making peace
by the blood of your cross,
~Be with us at the hour of our death.

Lord Jesus, lover of the human race,
~Be with us at the hour of our death.

Spontaneous prayers of intercession

Prayer

Leader: Abba, compassionate God,
          hear our prayers for our last days on earth.
          In your mercy relieve us of all our sins,
          strengthen our hope in you,
          and make us fully confident of the salvation
          you have sealed for us in the Holy Spirit.
          We ask this through Christ our Lord.

All: *~Amen.*

Alternative Prayer

Leader: Lord Jesus Christ,
you want everyone's salvation
and no one ever appeals to you in vain,
for with your own lips you promised:
"Whatever you ask the Father in my name,
I will do."
In your name — Jesus-Savior —
I ask that in my dying moments
you will give me full use of my senses,
heart-felt sorrow for my sins,
firm faith, hope in good measure,
and perfect love,
that I may be able to say honestly to you:
"Into your hands, O Lord, I commend my spirit.
You have redeemed me, Lord God of truth."

All: ~Amen.

— St. Vincent Ferrer (1350–1419)

Blessing

Leader: May Christ, the Lord of the living and the dead,
+ bring us in safety to our heavenly home.

All: ~Amen.

❧ AT THE DEATH OF A CHRISTIAN – I

Christian custom dictates that we remember and pray for our dead
friends and relatives at wakes and funerals, on their anniversaries
each year, and, in a very special way, on November 2, the feast of
All Souls. "It is a holy and wholesome thought to pray for the dead,
that they may be loosed from their sins" (2 Maccabees 12:46).

Leader: In the name of Jesus +
who will come again in glory
to judge the living and the dead.

All: ~Amen.

Hymn

May God the Father look on you with love,
and call you to himself in bliss above.
May God the Son, good Shepherd of his sheep,
stretch out his hand and waken you from sleep.
May God the Spirit breathe on you his peace,
where joys beyond all knowing never cease.

May flights of angels lead you on your way
to paradise and heaven's eternal day!
May martyrs greet you after death's dark night,
and bid you enter into Zion's light!
May choirs of angels sing you to your rest
with once poor Lazarus, now for ever blest!

— Text: *In paradisum,* trans. James Quinn, S.J., *Praise for All
Seasons* (Kingston, N.Y.: Selah Publishing Co., 1994), p. 68

Psalm 90:1–6, 10, 12, 14–17
A PRAYER OF MOSES, GOD'S CHOSEN

Antiphon: Blessed are the dead who die in the Lord.

Lord, you have been our dwelling place
in all generations.
Before the mountains were brought forth,
or ever you had formed the earth and the world,
from everlasting to everlasting you are God.

You turn us back to the dust,
and say, "Turn back, you mortals!"
For a thousand years in your sight
are as yesterday when it is past,
or as a watch in the night.

You sweep them away; they are like a dream,
like grass which is renewed in the morning:
in the morning it flourishes and is renewed;
in the evening it fades and withers.

The years of our life are threescore and ten,
or if we are strong fourscore;
yet their span is but toil and trouble;
they are soon gone, and we fly away.

So teach us to number our days
that we may receive a heart of wisdom.
Satisfy us in the morning with your steadfast love,
that we may rejoice and be glad all our days.

Let your work be manifest to your servants,
and your glorious power to their children.
Let the favor of the Lord our God be upon us,
and establish the work of your hands;
yes, establish the work of your hands.

Eternal rest grant to them, O Lord,

and let perpetual light shine upon them.

Antiphon: Blessed are the dead who die in the Lord.

Prayer

> *Leader:* Let us pray (*pause for quiet prayer*)
>
> > Blessed are you, Author of the universe,
> > you make and you unmake,
> > you give life and permit death.
> > Stand in the center of our lives
> > and be our consoler and friend
> > as we say farewell to those we cherish.
> > We ask this through Christ our Lord.
>
> *All:* ~Amen.

Alternative Psalm COMFORT IN BEING KNOWN *Psalm 139:1–12*

Antiphon: I know that my Redeemer lives
and in my flesh I shall see God.

O Lord, you have searched me and known me!
You know when I sit down and when I rise up;
you discern my thoughts from afar.

You search out my path and my lying down,
and are acquainted with all my ways.
Even before a word is on my tongue, O Lord,
you know it completely.

You pursue me behind and before,
and lay your hand upon me.
Such knowledge is too wonderful for me;
it is so high, I cannot attain it.

Where shall I go from your spirit?
Or where shall I flee from your presence?
If I ascend to heaven, you are there!
If I make my bed in Sheol, you are there!

If I take the wings of the morning
and dwell in the deepest parts of the sea,
even there your hand shall lead me,
and your right hand shall hold me.

If I say, "Let only darkness cover me,
and the light about me be night,"
even the darkness is not dark to you,
the night is bright as day;
for darkness is as light to you.

Eternal rest grant to them, O Lord,

and let perpetual light shine upon them.

Antiphon: I know that my Redeemer lives
            and in my flesh I shall see God.

Prayer

Leader: Let us pray (*pause for quiet prayer*)

           Lord Jesus Christ, King of glory,
           deliver the souls of your faithful departed
           from the pains of death and hell.
           Rescue them from the lion's mouth
           and do not let them fall into darkness.
           May your standard-bearer Michael
           lead them into the holy light
           which you promised to Abraham
           and to his descendants for ever.
           You live and reign through all the ages of ages.

All: ~Amen.

First Reading   LORD OF LIFE AND DEATH   *Romans 14:7–9*

We do not live to ourselves, and we do not die to ourselves. If we live, we live to the Lord, and if we die, we die to the Lord; so then, whether we live or whether we die, we are the Lord's. For to this end Christ died and lived again, so that he might be Lord of both the dead and the living.

Responsory   *1 Corinthians 15:20, 27*

Leader: Christ has been raised from the dead.

All: *~Christ has been raised from the dead.*

The first fruits of those who have died.
~Christ has been raised from the dead.

God has put all things in subjection under his feet.
~Christ has been raised from the dead.

Eternal rest grant to them, O Lord.
~Christ has been raised from the dead.

Gospel Reading
THE RESURRECTION AND THE LIFE   *John 11:17, 20–27*

When Jesus arrived he found that Lazarus had already been in the tomb four days.... When Martha heard that Jesus was coming, she went and met him, while Mary stayed at home. Martha said to Jesus, "Lord, if you had been here, my brother would not have died. But even now I know that God will give you whatever you ask of him." Jesus said to her, "Your brother will rise again." Martha said to him, "I know that he will rise again in the resurrection on the last day." Jesus said to her, "I am the resurrection and the life. Those who believe in me, even though they die, will live, and everyone who lives and believes in me will never die. Do you believe this?" She said to him, "Yes, Lord, I believe that you are the Messiah, the Son of God, the one coming into the world."

Reflection

- Christ is the Lord of life and death.
- He claimed us in baptism and ever since.
- He is our living and loving Redeemer, now and always.

Response

Leader: From the gates of death, O Lord,

All: *~Deliver this faithful soul.*

Canticle of Simeon   *Luke 2:29–32*

Antiphon: Blest be the living God who reigns for ever!

Now, Lord, you let your servant go in peace:
your word has been fulfilled.

My own eyes have seen the salvation
which you have prepared in the sight of every people:

a light to reveal you to the nations
and the glory of your people Israel.

Eternal rest grant to them, O Lord,

and let perpetual light shine upon them.

Antiphon: Blest be the living God who reigns for ever!

Litany

Leader: Out of the depths we cry to you, O Lord;

All: *~Lord, hear our prayer.*

May your ears be attentive
~To the voice of our pleading.

From the gates of death,
~Deliver their souls, O Lord.

May they rest in peace.
~Amen.

O Lord, hear our prayer,
~And let our cry come before you.

Prayer

Leader: Grant eternal rest, O Christ,
to your servant, N_____ ,
where suffering and pain exist no more
and where there is no more sighing or grieving.

Immortal One, maker of humankind,
be generous to your own creation,
forgive their fragile nature
and wipe away all their sins
by your overflowing mercy.
You, O Christ, are the life and the light of the world,
now and for ever.

All: ~*Amen.*

Alternative Prayer

Leader: O Savior and lover of the human race,
Prince of life immortal,
your death frees us from the fear of death,
your grave yields up forgiveness for all,
and your light illumines the world of shadows.
As the demons fall prostrate before you,
unite us with the rejoicing angels
and the exulting saints of every time and place
and conduct us with them
to your Paradise for ever green,
where you live and reign in risen glory,
now and always and for ever and ever.

All: ~*Amen.*

— After Hippolytus of Rome (ca. 165–235), trans. Walter Mitchell
in *Divine Inspiration* (New York: Oxford University Press, 1998),
p. 264, alt.

Blessing

Leader: Eternal rest grant to them, O Lord,

All: ~*And let perpetual light shine upon them.*

May their souls and the souls
of all the faithful departed
through the mercy of God + rest in peace.
~*Amen.*

◈ AT THE DEATH OF A CHRISTIAN – II

Leader: Holy is God, + holy and strong,
holy and living for ever.

All: ~*Lord, have mercy.*

Hymn

O radiant Light, O Sun divine
Of God the Father's deathless face,
O Image of the light sublime
That fills the heavenly dwelling place:

O Son of God, the source of life,
Praise is your due by night and day;
Our happy lips must raise the strain
Of your esteemed and splendid name.

Lord Jesus Christ, as daylight fades,
As shine the lights of eventide,
We praise the Father with the Son,
The Spirit blest and with them one. Amen.

> — Text: *Phos hilaron,* Greek, 2nd–3rd century,
> trans. William G. Storey

Canticle of Isaiah   *Isaiah 26:1–4, 9, 12, 19*

Antiphon: O dwellers in the dust,
awake and sing for joy!

We have a strong city;
God sets up victory
like walls and bulwarks.
Open the gates
so that the righteous nation
that keeps faith
may enter in.

Those of steadfast mind you keep in peace —
in peace because they trust in you.
Trust in the Lord for ever,
for in the Lord God
you have an everlasting rock.

My soul yearns for you in the night,
my spirit within me earnestly seeks you.
For when your judgments are in the earth,
the inhabitants of the world learn righteousness.
O Lord, you will ordain peace for us,
for indeed, all that we have done,
you have done for us.

Your dead shall live,
their corpses shall rise.
O dwellers in the dust,
awake and sing for joy!
For your dew is a radiant dew,
and the earth will give birth
to those long dead.

Eternal rest grant to them, O Lord,

and let perpetual light shine upon them.

Antiphon: O dwellers in the dust,
            awake and sing for joy!

Prayer

Leader: Let us pray (*pause for quiet prayer*)

God of love,
have mercy on our brothers and sisters
who have died in the faith of Christ.
May these dwellers in the dust
awake and sing for joy in your presence,
through all eternity.

All: ~Amen.

First Reading   YOU ARE MINE   *Isaiah 43:1–4*

Thus says the Lord who made you, who formed you in the womb
and will help you: Do not fear, for I have redeemed you; I have
called you by name, you are mine. When you pass through the
waters, I will be with you; and through the rivers, they shall not
overwhelm you; when you walk through fire you shall not be
burned, and the flame shall not consume you. For I am the Lord

your God, the Holy One of Israel, your Savior. Because you are precious in my sight, and honored, and I love you.

Responsory   *Isaiah 44: 3, 4*

> *Leader:* I will pour water on the thirsty land,
> and streams on the dry ground.
>
> > *All:* ~*I will pour water on the thirsty land,*
> > *and streams on the dry ground.*
> >
> > I will pour my Spirit upon your descendants.
> > ~*And streams on the dry ground.*
> >
> > You shall spring up like willows
> > by flowing streams.
> > ~*And streams on the dry ground.*
> >
> > Eternal rest grant to them, O Lord.
> > ~*I will pour water on the thirsty land,*
> > *and streams on the dry ground.*

Second Reading   CHRISTIAN HOPE   *1 Thessalonians 4:13–18*

Our friends, we want you to know the truth about those who have died, so that you will not be sad, as are those who have no hope. We believe that Jesus died and rose again, and so we believe that God will take back with Jesus those who have died believing in him. What we are teaching you now is the Lord's teaching: we who are alive on the day the Lord comes will not go ahead of those who have died. There will be the shout of command, the archangel's voice, the sound of God's trumpet, and the Lord himself will come down from heaven. Those who have died believing in Christ will rise to life first; then we who are living at that time will be gathered up along with them in the clouds to meet the Lord in the air. And so we will always be with the Lord. So then, encourage one another with these words.

Reflection

- God is with us as we pass through the waters of death.

- We are precious in his sight.

- He saves us and gives us hope through Jesus.

Response

> *Leader:*   Be faithful unto death,

> *All:*   ~*And I will give you the crown of life.*

Canticle of Brother Sun and Sister Moon

Most high, almighty, good Lord!
All praise, glory, honor, and exaltation are yours!
To you alone do they belong,
and no mere mortal dares pronounce your name.
~*We praise you, O Lord!*

Praise to you, O Lord our God, for all your creatures:
first, for our dear Brother Sun,
who gives us the day
and illumines us with his light;
fair is he, in splendor radiant,
bearing your very likeness, O Lord.
~*We praise you, O Lord!*

For our Sister Moon,
and for the bright, shining stars:
~*We praise you, O Lord!*

For our Brother Wind,
for fair and stormy seasons
and all heaven's varied moods,
by which you nourish all that you have made:
~*We praise you, O Lord!*

For our Sister Water,
so useful, lowly, precious and pure:
~*We praise you, O Lord!*

For our Brother Fire,
who brightens up our darkest nights:
beautiful is he and eager,
invincible and keen:
~*We praise you, O Lord!*

For our Mother Earth,
who sustains and feeds us,
producing fair fruits,
and many-colored flowers and herbs:
~We praise you, O Lord!

For those who forgive one another for love of you,
and who patiently bear sickness and other trials.
— Happy are they who peacefully endure;
you will crown them, O Most high! —
~We praise you, O Lord!

For our sister Death,
the inescapable fact of life.
— Woe to those who die in mortal sin!
Happy those she finds doing your will!
From the Second Death they stand immune —
~We praise you, O Lord!

All creatures,
praise and glorify my Lord
and give him thanks
and serve him in great humility.
~We praise you, O Lord!

> — St. Francis of Assisi (1181–1226), trans. William G. Storey

Litany

Leader: Jesus, Savior of the world,

All: *~Grant them eternal rest.*

Jesus, good shepherd of the flock,
~Grant them eternal rest.

Jesus, the way, the truth, and the life,
~Grant them eternal rest.

Jesus, our resurrection and our life,
~Grant them eternal rest.

Jesus, the first-fruits of those
who have fallen asleep in death,
~Grant them eternal rest.

Jesus, the same, yesterday, today, and for ever,
~*Grant them eternal rest.*

Jesus, who will come again in glory
to judge the living and the dead,
~*Grant them eternal rest.*

Spontaneous prayers of intercession

Prayer

Leader: Creator and Redeemer,
Christ conquered death
and brought life to those in the grave.
May all who put their faith in him
and in the power of his resurrection
share in his glorious victory
and enjoy the radiant vision
of the holy and undivided Trinity,
in the community of all the saints,
for ever and ever.

All: ~*Amen.*

Alternative Prayer

Leader: May God support us all the day long,
till the shadows lengthen
and the evening comes
and the busy world is hushed
and the fever of life is over
and our work is done —
then in his mercy —
may he give us a safe lodging
and a holy rest
and peace at the last.

All: ~*Amen.*

— Attributed to John Henry Newman (1801–1890)

Blessing

Leader: Eternal rest grant to them, O Lord,

All: *~And let perpetual light shine upon them.*

May their souls and the souls
of all the faithful departed,
through the mercy of God, + rest in peace.
~Amen.

Immediately after death, the friends gathered at the deathbed may want to repeat one of the above devotions.

Five

LITANIES

The litanies in common use have several origins. They were first composed for daily morning and evening prayer, for the celebration of the Eucharist on the Lord's Day, and for processions. Later on some were arranged for more private, devotional uses. In each case they were designed to encourage and stimulate prayer of petition, an expression of confidence in Jesus' exhortation:

> "Ask, and you will receive;
> Seek, and you will find;
> Knock and the door will be opened to you."
>   (Matthew 7:7)

Litanies are being used in many churches today. In addition to this section, they are provided frequently in chapters 2 and 4. Many people find them helpful for special occasions, for prayers of intercession, for triduums (three days of prayer), for novenas (nine days of prayer), and for other times, such as that of serious illness, death, and dying.

ᚉ LITANY TO CHRIST OUR LORD

Leader: Jesus says:
I am the bread of life.
I am the bread that came down from heaven.
If you eat this bread,
you will live for ever. (John 6:35, 41, 51)

All: ~*Lord, give us this bread always.* (John 6:34)

Jesus says:
I am the vine,
and you are the branches.
Whoever remains in me will bear much fruit,
for you can do nothing without me. (John 15:5)
~*Lord, we believe you are the Holy One
who has come from God.* (John 6:69)

Jesus says:
I am the gate.
Whoever comes in by me will be saved. (John 10:9)
~*Lord, Lord! Let us in!* (Matthew 25:11)

Jesus says:
I am the light of the world.
Whoever follows me will have the light of life
and will never walk in darkness. (John 8:12)
~*Send us your light and your truth.* (Psalm 43:3)

Jesus says:
I am the good shepherd.
I know my sheep and they know me.
And I am willing to die for them. (John 10:14–15)
~*Lord, make us one flock with one shepherd.* (John 10:16)

Jesus says:
I am the resurrection and the life.
Whoever lives and believes in me
will never die. (John 11:25–26)
~*Lord, I do believe that you are the Messiah,
the Son of God.* (John 11:25)

Jesus says:
I am the way, the truth and the life;
no one goes to the Father except by me. (John 14:6)
~*Teach me your ways, O Lord.* (Psalm 25:4)

Jesus says:
I am the one who knows
everyone's thoughts and wishes.
I will repay each one of you
according to what you have done. (Revelation 2:22)
~*Examine me, O God, and know my heart.* (Psalm 139:27)

Jesus says:
I am descended from the family of David;
I am the bright morning star. (Revelation 22:16)
~*Son of David, have mercy on me!* (Matthew 15:22)

Jesus says:
I am the Alpha and the Omega,
the beginning and the end,
the first and the last. (Revelation 22:13)
~*Lord, you show us that the first shall be last
and the last first.* (Matthew 19:30)

Prayer

Leader: Lord Jesus Christ,
the world's true sun,
ever rising, never setting,
whose life-giving warmth
engenders, preserves,
nourishes, and gladdens
all things in heaven and on earth:
shine in my soul, I pray,
scatter the night of sin,
and the clouds of error.
Blaze within me,
that I may go my way without stumbling,
taking no part in the shameful deeds
of those who wander in the dark,
but all my life long
walking as one native to the light.

All: ~*Amen.*

— *Desiderius Erasmus* (1467–1536)

❧ LITANY OF THE HOLY NAME OF JESUS

Leader: Lord, have mercy.

All: ~*Lord, have mercy.*

Christ, have mercy.
~*Christ, have mercy.*

Lord, have mercy.
~*Lord have mercy.*

God our Father in heaven,
~*Have mercy on us.*

God the Son, Redeemer of the world,
~*Have mercy on us.*

God the Holy Spirit,
~*Have mercy on us.*

Holy Trinity, one God,
~*Have mercy on us.*

Jesus, Son of the living God,
~*Have mercy on us.*

Jesus, splendor of the Father,
Jesus, brightness of everlasting light,
Jesus, king of glory,
Jesus, dawn of justice,
Jesus, Son of the Virgin Mary,
Jesus, worthy of our love,
Jesus, worthy of our wonder,
Jesus, mighty God,
Jesus, father of the world to come,
Jesus, prince of peace,
Jesus, all-powerful,
Jesus, pattern of patience,
Jesus, model of obedience,
Jesus, gentle and humble of heart,

Jesus, lover of chastity,
Jesus, lover of us all,
Jesus, God of peace,

Jesus, author of life,
Jesus, model of goodness,
Jesus, seeker of souls,
Jesus, our God,
Jesus, our refuge,
Jesus, father of the poor,
Jesus, treasure of the faithful,

Jesus, good shepherd,
Jesus, the true light,
Jesus, eternal wisdom,
Jesus, infinite goodness,
Jesus, our way and our life,
Jesus, joy of angels,
Jesus, king of patriarchs,
Jesus, teacher of apostles,
Jesus, master of evangelists,
Jesus, courage of martyrs,
Jesus, light of confessors,
Jesus, purity of virgins,
Jesus, crown of all saints,

Lord, be merciful,
~*Jesus, save your people.*

From all evil,
From every sin,
From the snares of the devil,
From your anger,
From the spirit of infidelity,
From everlasting death,
From neglect of your Holy Spirit,

By the mystery of your incarnation,
By your birth,
By your childhood,
By your hidden life,
By your public ministry,
By your agony and crucifixion,
By your abandonment,
By your grief and sorrow,
By your death and burial,

By your rising to new life,
By your return in glory to the Father,
By your gift of the holy Eucharist,
By your joy and glory,

Christ, hear us.
~*Christ, hear us.*

Lord Jesus, hear our prayer.
~*Lord Jesus, hear our prayer.*

Lamb of God, you take away the sins of the world,
~*Have mercy on us.*

Lamb of God, you take away the sins of the world,
~*Have mercy on us.*

Lamb of God, you take away the sins of the world,
~*Have mercy on us.*

Prayer

Leader: Let us pray (*pause for intercessions*)

Lord, may we who honor the holy name of Jesus
enjoy his friendship in this life
and be filled with eternal joy in the kingdom
where he lives and reigns for ever and ever.

All: ~*Amen.*

— *A Book of Prayers* (Washington, D.C.: ICEL, 1982), pp. 21–23

◎ LITANY OF THE BEATITUDES

Leader: Lord Jesus, teacher of righteousness;

All: ~*Give us true happiness and every blessing.*

Bless the poor and humble in spirit;
~*Make them inherit the kingdom of heaven.*

Bless those who mourn for lost blessings;
~*Be their comfort in time of trouble.*

Bless those who are meek and humble of heart;
~*Let them inherit what God has promised.*

Bless those who hunger and thirst
for what God requires;
~And fill them with divine wholeness.

Bless those who are merciful toward others;
~May God be merciful to them in turn.

Bless those who are pure in heart;
~Let them see God in the light of glory.

Bless those who make peace on earth;
~And call them the children of God.

Bless those who are persecuted for being holy;
~Give them possession of the kingdom of God.

Bless those who are slandered and insulted
for your sake;
*~Make them happy and glad for their reward is great
in their heavenly home.*

Spontaneous prayers of intercession

Prayer

Leader: O God, giver of all blessings,
your dear Son taught us how to be happy,
in this life and in the next,
by walking in his blessed footsteps.
Make us humble, pure and merciful;
help us to make peace and pursue holiness
and to rejoice when we are persecuted,
slandered and insulted for his sake.
We ask this in his holy name.

All: *~Amen.*

௸ **LITANY TO THE HOLY SPIRIT**

Leader: Come, Spirit of wisdom, and teach us
             to value the highest gift.

All: ~*Come, Holy Spirit.*

         Come, Spirit of understanding,
         and show us all things in the light of eternity.
         ~*Come, Holy Spirit.*

         Come, Spirit of counsel,
         and guide us along the straight and narrow path
         to our heavenly home.
         ~*Come, Holy Spirit.*

         Come, Spirit of might, and strengthen us
         against every evil spirit and interest
         which would separate us from you.
         ~*Come, Holy Spirit.*

         Come, Spirit of knowledge, and teach us
         the shortness of life and the length of eternity.
         ~*Come, Holy Spirit.*

         Come Spirit of godliness,
         and stir up our minds and hearts
         to love and serve the Lord our God all our days.
         ~*Come, Holy Spirit.*

         Come, Spirit of the fear of the Lord,
         and make us tremble with awe and reverence
         before your divine majesty.
         ~*Come, Holy Spirit.*

         Send forth your Spirit and they shall be created.
         ~*And you shall renew the face of the earth.*

         Let us pray (*pause for quiet prayer*)

         Holy Spirit of truth,
         Sovereign Lord of the universe,
         guide and guardian of your people,
         present everywhere,
         overflowing all that exists:

come and live in us,
cleanse us from all sin,
pour out your blessings on us,
give us fresh life,
and in your gracious love
bring us to salvation.

All: ~*Amen.*

✸ LITANY OF PRAISE AND THANKSGIVING

Leader: O God, our heavenly Father,
the giver of every good and perfect gift,
we lift up to you our voice in thanksgiving;
we praise you for the life you have given us,
and for the service to which you have appointed us,
for the knowledge of your will,
and the inspiration of your love:

All: ~*We praise you, O God.*

For the work we have strength to do,
for the truth we are permitted to learn;
for whatever good there has been in our past lives,
and for the hope that leads us on to better things:
~*We thank you, O God.*

For revealing your presence in nature,
and the tokens of your wisdom and power,
in the least as in the greatest;
for every moment of closer communion with your Spirit
in all that is fair and glorious in the universe:
~*We thank you, O God.*

For home and friends,
for all the comfort and gladness of our lives;
for encouragement to duty,
for help in time of temptation;
for sympathy in sorrow,
for the peace that is gained through strife,
and the rest that comes after toil:
~*We thank you, O God.*

Make us worthy of all your mercies,
and give us the grace to know and do your holy will,
so may your kingdom come, and your will be done,
on earth as it is in heaven.
~*Amen.*

O God, infinite Ruler of creation,
you divide day from darkness
and turn the shadow of death into morning;
drive out all wrong desires,
incline our hearts to keep your law,
and guide our feet into the way of peace;
having done your will with cheerfulness
while it was day
may we rejoice in thanking you as night comes on;
we ask this through Christ Jesus, our blessed Savior.
~*Amen.*

> — Text: Anon., *The Order of Evening Worship in the Meeting House on Star Island* (Boston: Merrymount Press, 1903), np; sl. alt.

≪ **GENERAL LITANY**

Leader: In peace, let us pray to the Lord.

All: ~*Lord, hear our prayer.*

For peace from on high
and for the salvation of our souls,
let us pray to the Lord.
~*Lord, hear our prayer.*

For the welfare of the one, holy,
catholic, and apostolic church
and for the unity of the human race,
let us pray to the Lord.
~*Lord, hear our prayer.*

For the ministers of the Gospel
who serve God in faith and love,
let us pray to the Lord.
~*Lord, hear our prayer.*

For this nation, its government,
and for all who serve and protect us,
let us pray to the Lord.
~*Lord, hear our prayer.*

For this city, and for every city and country,
and for all those living in them, let us pray to the Lord.
~*Lord, hear our prayer.*

For seasonable weather, for bountiful harvests,
and for the poor who set their hope in God,
let us pray to the Lord.
~*Lord, hear our prayer.*

For the safety of travelers, the recovery of the sick,
the deliverance of the oppressed,
and the release of prisoners, let us pray to the Lord.
~*Lord, hear our prayer.*

For those who have fallen asleep in Christ,
especially *N*_____,
let us pray to the Lord.
~*Lord, hear our prayer.*

For those whom we call to mind today, *N*_____,
let us pray to the Lord.
~*Lord, hear our prayer.*

For a part and inheritance in the glorious company
of all the saints,
Let us pray to the Lord.
~*Lord, hear our prayer.*

Help, save, pity, and defend us, O God, by your grace.

Spontaneous prayers of intercession

Leader: In the communion of the Holy Spirit,
let us commend ourselves, one another,
and our whole life to Christ our Lord.

All: ~*To you, O Lord.*

Prayer

Leader: Holy and mighty God,
you hear the beating of every human heart.
May our prayers ascend before you like incense
and may your loving kindness descend upon us
like the dew of heaven
to refresh and restore us day by day.
In Jesus' name.

All: ~*Amen.*

— Adapted from the Byzantine Liturgy

Acknowledgments

Acknowledgment is gratefully extended for permission to reprint the following:

Scripture readings and Canticles are from the New Revised Standard Version Bible, copyright © 1989 by the Division of Christian Education of the National Council of the Churches of Christ in the U.S.A., published by Thomas Nelson Publishers; from the Good News Translation in Today's English Version – Second Edition Copyright © 1992 by American Bible Society; or from *A New Zealand Prayer Book*, William Collins Publishers Ltd., © 1989. Used with permission.

The Psalms are taken from *Psalms for Praise and Worship*, edited and prepared by John C. Holbert et al., Abingdon Press, © 1992.

"A Wedding Toast" from *The Mind-Reader*, copyright © 1972 by Richard Wilbur, reprinted by permission of Harcourt, Inc.

"Cana" by Thomas Merton, from *The Collected Poems of Thomas Merton*, copyright © 1946 by New Directions Publishing Corporation, 1977 by the Trustees of the Merton Legacy Trust. Reprinted by permission of New Directions Publishing Corp.

"Hail Our Savior's Glorious Body; "May God the Father Look on Us with Love; "At This Same Hour, Redeemer King"; "O Sacred Heart for All Once Broken"; "Father of Mercies," by James Quinn, S.J., *Praise for All Seasons*. Kingston, N.Y.: Selah Publishing Co., 1994. Used with permission.

Prayers by Ida N. Munson and Joseph Mary Plunkett from *Christ in Poetry*, ed. Thomas C. Clark and Hazel D. Clark (New York: Association Press, 1952).

"Magnificat," trans. Owen Alstott © 1993 Oregon Catholic Press.

"Blest Be the God of Israel." Words: Carl P. Daw, Jr. Words © 1989 by Hope Publishing Co., Carol Stream, IL 60188. All rights reserved. Used by permission.

"O God Beyond All Praising." Words: Michel Perry. Words © 1982, 1987 by Jubilate Hymns, Ltd. (admin. by Hope Publishing Company, Carol Stream, IL 60188). All rights reserved. Used by permission.

"Hymn to the Holy Spirit" (*Veni, Creator Spiritus*), trans. John Webster Grant, copyright John Webster Grant, from *The Hymn Book of the Anglican Church of Canada* (1971), #246.

"The Setting Sun Now Dies Away" (*Iam sol recedit igneus*), trans. Geoffrey Laycock, based on *The Primer*, 1706, © Faber Music Ltd.; adapted by Ralph Wright, O.S.B., © GIA Publications, Inc., Chicago, Illinois. All rights reserved. Used with permission.

OF RELATED INTEREST
BY THOMAS KEATING

---■---

AWAKENINGS

An examination of the key events in the ministry of Jesus, the important parables, and the many celebrations of his presence in light of today's experience of living.

0-8245-1044-5; $12.95 paperback

REAWAKENINGS

Further Gospel explorations from America's leading contemplative.

0-8245-1149-2; $14.95 paperback

THE KINGDOM OF GOD IS LIKE . . .

"A useful book to aid our own reading of biblical texts in a contemplative style that constantly opens us up to new levels of meaning." — *Monos*

0-8245-1659-1; $14.95 paperback

THE HEART OF THE WORLD

"The reader's introduction to contemplative Christianity will result in his or her eternal friendship with it." — *The Liguorian*

0-8245-0903-X; $9.95 paperback

---■---

crossroad

BEYOND THE MIRROR
Reflections on Death and Life

"This small work may be Henri Nouwen's most honest and insightful.... That is saying quite a bit when one considers the prolific output by the late spiritual writer."   — Critical Review Service

Beyond the Mirror, about Nouwen's near death experience in 1989, has been unavailable since 1997. This new edition includes a foreword by Robert Durback and an afterword from the Henri Nouwen Archives about preparing for death.

0-8245-1961-2; $14.95 paperback

FINDING MY WAY HOME
Pathways to Life and the Spirit

A collection of four essays, three previously published by Crossroad and here revised, that examines four different aspects of our spiritual life: the Path of Waiting, the Path of Power, the Path of Peace, and the Path of Living and Dying (never before published in book form).

0-8245-1888-8; $18.95 hardcover

SABBATICAL JOURNEY
The Diary of His Final Year

Now in paperback! "Sabbatical Journey is must reading for Nouwen fans and a fine introduction to the man for the uninitiated.... This journal reveals much about the heart and mind of a theologian who has touched the lives of millions...."   — *Commonweal*

0-8245-1878-0; $15.95 paperback

crossroad

Dick Ryan, Editor

STRAIGHT FROM THE HEART
Reflections from Twentieth Century Mystics

A collection of wise sayings, profound proverbs, and deep wisdom on a variety of spiritual themes from the best-known mystics of the twentieth century, including Joyce Rupp, Henri Nouwen, Miriam Therese Winter, and Thomas Merton.

0-8245-1923-X; $19.95 hardcover

Simon Parke

ORIGINS
For Those Bored with the Shallow End

"When profound, intelligent, and witty go together, you know you have someone worth listening to! This wonderful collection of quick, readable 'parables' will stay with you for a long time — and lead you out of the shallows." — Richard Rohr, O.F.M.

0-8245-1910-8; $16.95 hardcover

Robert Kirschner

DIVINE THINGS
Seeking the Sacred in a Secular Age

"Kirschner's lively, up-to-date, and wonderfully rich presentation of the ancient wisdom of the Hebrew Scriptures will enliven and enlighten the lives of all readers." — M. Basil Pennington, O.C.S.O.

0-8245-1897-7; $14.95 paperback

crossroad